INCREDIBLE
Origami

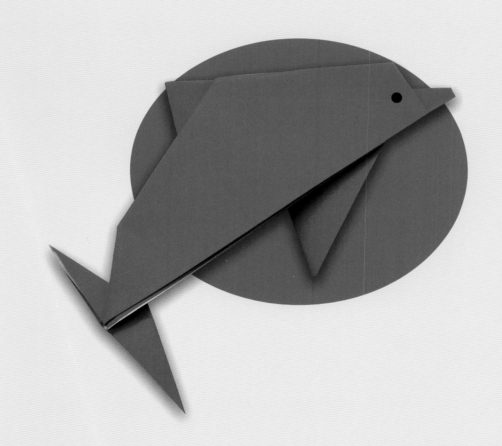

ARCTURUS

ARCTURUS

This edition published in 2020 by Arcturus Publishing Limited
26/27 Bickels Yard, 151–153 Bermondsey Street,
London SE1 3HA

Models and photography by Belinda Webster, Michael Wiles, and
Jessica Moon
Text by Lisa Miles, Jennifer Saunderson, and Catherine Ard
Design by Picnic Design, Emma Randall, Jessica Moon, and Steve Flight
Edited by Anna Brett, Becca Clunes, Sarah Eason, Kate Overy, Joe Fullman,
and Frances Evans
Picture credits: Shutterstock, Cristobal Garciaferro 117br, Bomshtein 153 br

ISBN: 978-1-78428-855-6
CH004797NT
Supplier 29, Date 0120, Print run 9998

Printed in China

Contents

Introduction

Origami models often share the same folds and basic designs, known as "bases." This introduction explains the ones you will need for the projects in this book. When making the models, follow the key below to find out what the lines and arrows mean.

KEY

valley fold   - - - - - - - - - - - - - - -

mountain fold   • • • • • • • • • • • • • • •

hold paper in place with finger

step fold (mountain and valley fold next to each other)

direction to move paper

direction to push or pull

MOUNTAIN FOLD

To make a mountain fold, fold the paper so that the crease is pointing up at you, like a mountain.

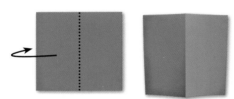

VALLEY FOLD

To make a valley fold, fold the paper the other way, so that the crease is pointing away from you, like a valley.

INSIDE REVERSE FOLD

An inside reverse fold is useful if you want to make a nose or a tail, or if you want to flatten the shape of another part of your model.

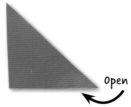
Open

1 First, fold a piece of paper diagonally in half. Make a valley fold on one point and crease.

2 It's important to make sure that the paper is creased well. Run your finger over the crease two or three times.

3 Unfold and open up the corner slightly. Refold the crease nearest to you into a mountain fold.

4 Open up the paper a little more and then tuck the tip of the point inside. Close the paper. This is the view from the underside of the paper.

5 Flatten the paper. You now have an inside reverse fold.

OUTSIDE REVERSE FOLD

An outside reverse fold is useful if you want to make a head, beak, or foot, or another part of your model that sticks out.

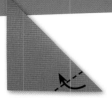   

open

1 First, fold a piece of paper diagonally in half. Make a valley fold on one point and crease.

2 It's important to make sure that the paper is creased well. Run your finger over the crease two or three times.

3 Unfold and open up the corner slightly. Refold the crease farthest away from you into a mountain fold.

4 Open up the paper a little more and start to turn the corner inside out. Then close the paper when the fold begins to turn.

5 You now have an outside reverse fold. You can either flatten the paper or leave it rounded out.

KITE BASE

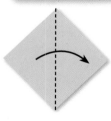 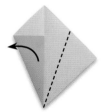 

1 Start with the paper like this. Valley fold it in half diagonally.

2 Valley fold the left section to meet the middle crease.

3 Do the same on the other side.

4 You now have a kite base.

BLINTZ BASE

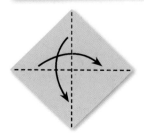 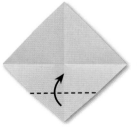 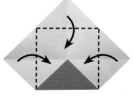

1 Start with the paper like this. Make two diagonal valley folds.

2 Now fold the bottom point up to the middle.

3 Repeat step 2 with the three remaining points.

4 You now have a blintz base.

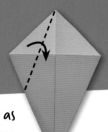

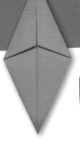

1 Make a kite base, as shown above. Valley fold the left corner.

2 Do the same on the other side.

3 The paper should now look like this.

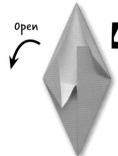

Open

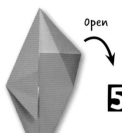

Open

4 Open out the top left corner. Take hold of the inside flap. Pull it down to meet the middle crease to make a new flap as shown.

5 Flatten the paper. Then do the same on the other side.

6 You now have a fish base.

SQUARE BASE

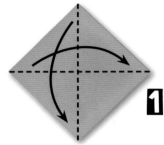

1 Start with a square of paper like this. Make two diagonal valley folds.

2 The paper should look like this. Now turn it over.

3 Valley fold along the horizontal and vertical lines.

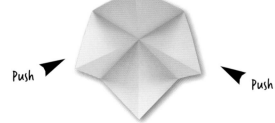

Push

Push

4 The paper should now look like this.

5 Hold the paper by opposite diagonal corners. Push the two corners together so that the shape begins to collapse.

6 Flatten the top of the paper into a square shape. You now have a square base.

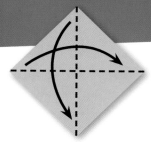

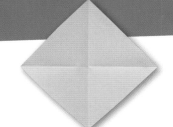

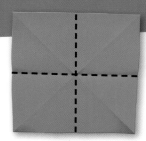

1 Start with a square of paper, with the point facing you. Make two diagonal valley folds.

2 The paper should now look like this. Turn it over.

3 Make two valley folds along the horizontal and vertical lines.

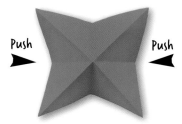

Push   Push

4 Push the paper into this shape, so the middle spot pops up.

5 Push in the sides, so that the back and front sections are brought together.

6 Flatten the paper. You now have a waterbomb base.

BIRD BASE

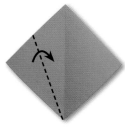

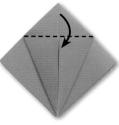

1 Start with a square base, as shown on page 6, with the open end nearest to you. Valley fold the top left flap to the middle crease.

2 Do the same on the other side.

3 Valley fold the top triangle.

4 Unfold the top and sides and you have the shape shown here.

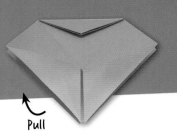

Pull

5 Take the bottom corner and begin to open out the upper flap by gently pulling up.

6 The paper should open like a bird's beak. Open out the flap as far as it will go.

7 Flatten the paper so that you now have this shape. Turn the paper over.

8 The paper should now look like this. Repeat steps 1 to 7 on this side.

9 You now have a bird base. The two flaps at the bottom are separated by an open slit.

ORGAN BASE

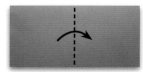

1 Start with a square of paper white side up. Valley fold the paper in half from top to bottom.

2 Valley fold the paper in half again from the left to the right, crease well, and then unfold.

3 Valley fold the left side into the middle.

4 Valley fold the right side into the middle.

Open

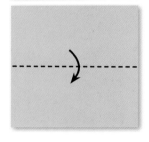

Press

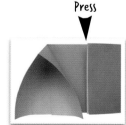

5 Unfold the left flap and open it up.

6 Press the top down to flatten the left side.

7 The paper should now look like this. Repeat steps 5 and 6 on the right side.

8 You now have an organ base. The two flaps at the bottom are separated by an open slit.

ORIGAMI FASHION FOLDS

STEP FOLD

The step fold creates a zigzag, or step, in the paper. It is used to divide different parts of a garment, such as the skirt and bodice of a dress.

1 First fold a piece of paper in half from bottom to top, then unfold.

2 Now make a mountain fold above the valley fold you just made.

3 Push the mountain fold over the valley fold and press it flat.

4 You now have a step fold.

A step fold like the one here, with the mountain fold above the valley fold, is shown like this.

A step fold with the mountain fold below the valley fold is shown like this.

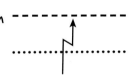

PLEAT FOLD

Once you have mastered a step fold, making a pleat is easy. In the Origami fashion chapter, step folds are always horizontal and pleats are vertical. A pleat fold uses some creases that have been made in earlier steps.

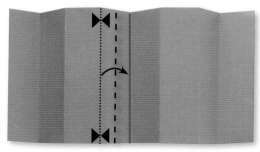

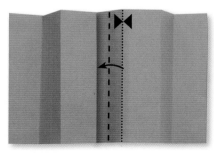

1 To make the first side of a pleat, pinch the crease shown between your fingers. Fold it over to the right until it lines up with the crease indicated. Press it flat to make a valley crease in the paper underneath.

2 Repeat on the other side. Pinch the crease shown and fold it over to the left until it lines up with the crease indicated. Press it flat to make a valley crease underneath.

Hold the paper up and the finished pleat will look like this from the side.

ORIGAMI ANIMALS

Sea creatures

In this chapter, find out how to make a wonderful origami underwater world, from a graceful dolphin to a dangerous ray with a sting in its tail!

Seal

Ray

Gulp!

Shark

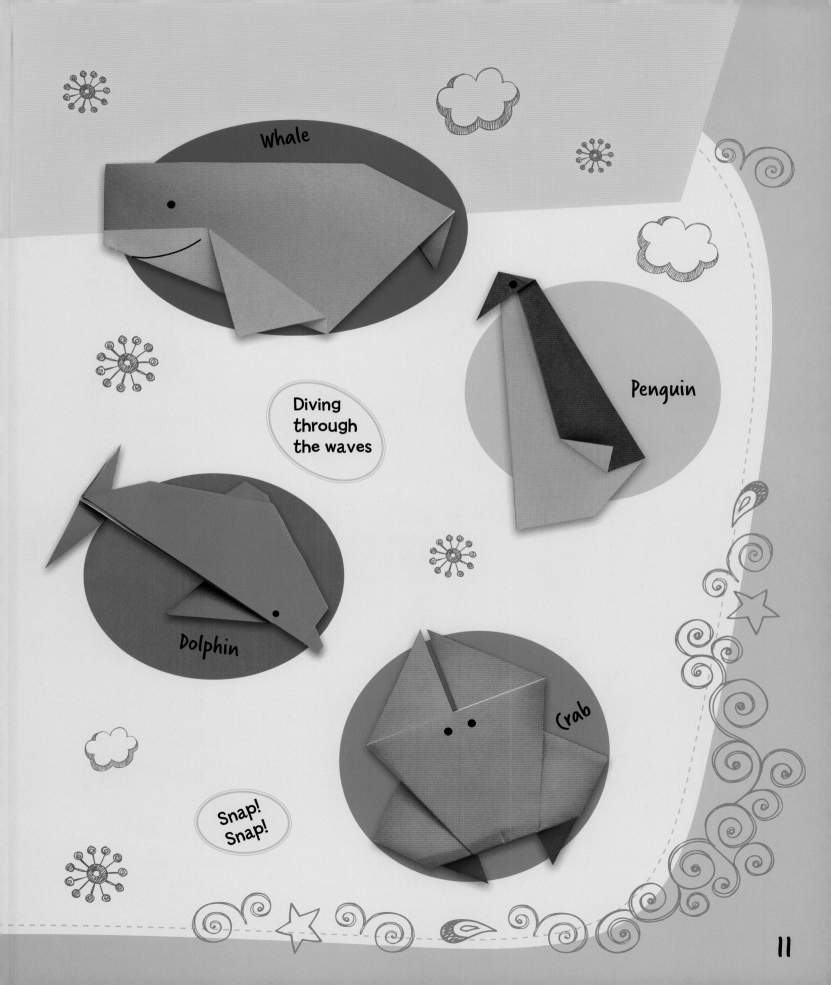

Whale

Penguin

Diving through the waves

Dolphin

Crab

Snap! Snap!

Penguin

The penguin is a brilliant swimmer but it waddles on land. So don't worry if your origami model wobbles — it just makes it more realistic!

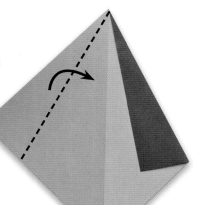

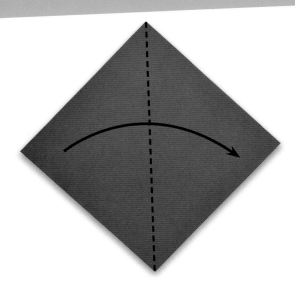

1 Turn the paper so one point is facing down. Valley fold it in half from left to right.

2 Open it out. Turn the paper over so that the crease becomes a mountain fold. Valley fold the right corner.

3 Do the same on the other side.

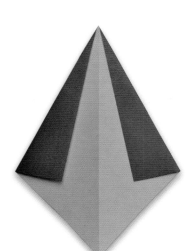

4 The paper should now look like this.

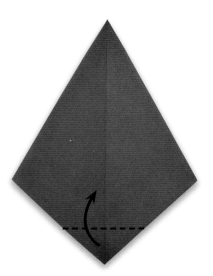

5 Turn the paper over and valley fold the bottom.

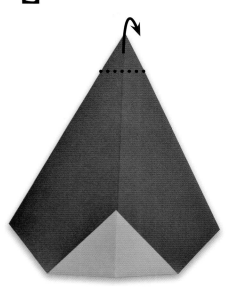

6 Mountain fold the top of the paper over.

7 Valley fold the paper in half from left to right.

8 Valley fold the corner tip. This is the penguin's wing. Do the same on the other side.

10 Stand up the model and your origami penguin is complete!

Pull

9 Now pull up the beak.

Whale

The blue whale is the biggest animal to have ever lived, bigger even than the largest dinosaur. A real one would be about 200 times longer than your model!

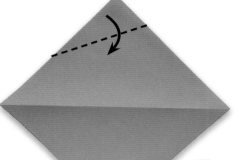

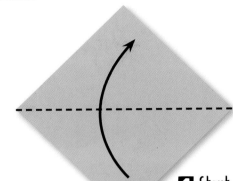

1 Start with the paper white side up with one point facing down. Valley fold in half from bottom to top.

2 Open the paper out. Turn it over, so that the middle crease is now a mountain fold. Fold down the top corner.

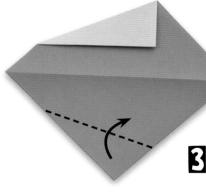

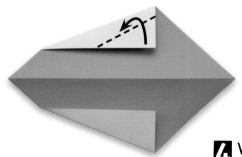

3 Do the same on the other side.

4 Valley fold the tip of the top corner.

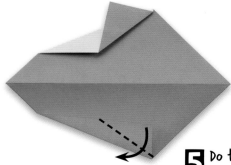

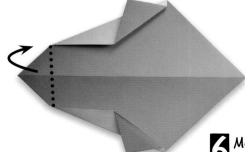

5 Do the same on the other side.

6 Mountain fold the left side of the paper.

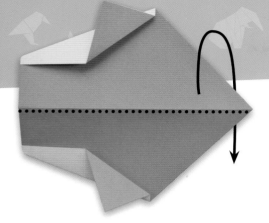

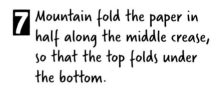

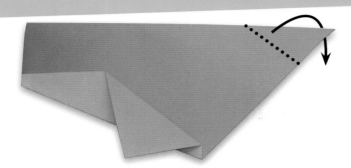

7 Mountain fold the paper in half along the middle crease, so that the top folds under the bottom.

8 Mountain fold the right corner. Unfold, then make an inside reverse fold to create the tail.

9

Now draw on a smiley face and you have an origami whale!

Seal

The seal is clumsy on land and uses its flippers to pull itself along. In the sea, though, it speeds through the water, twisting and turning.

START WITH A FISH BASE

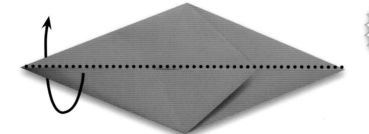

1 Find out how to make a fish base on page 6. With the flaps pointing right, fold it in half so that the bottom goes under the top section.

2 Mountain fold the left point.

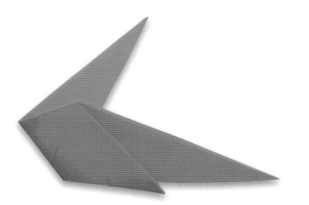

3 Unfold, then make an inside reverse fold to create the seal's neck.

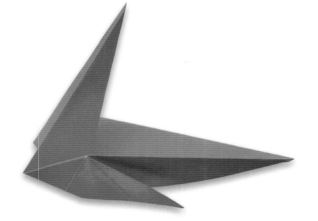

4 Looking from above, you should now be able to see the inside reverse fold, as shown above.

5 Mountain fold the top point.

16

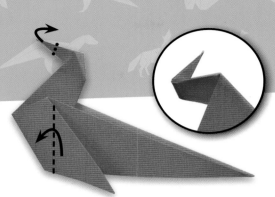

Close-up of head.

6 Unfold, then make an inside reverse fold to create the seal's head.

7 Valley fold the flippers forward on both sides. Mountain fold the tip of the seal's head.

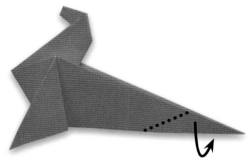

9 Unfold, then make an inside reverse fold to create the tail. On one of the flippers, valley fold the tip of the flap.

8 Unfold, then tuck in the seal's nose to make it blunt. Mountain fold the right point.

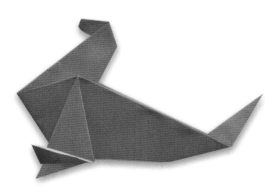

10 Valley fold the tip of the other flipper.

11 Now your origami seal is standing up and ready to clap its flippers!

Dolphin

Dolphins are supposed to bring good luck to sailors.
Maybe this origami version will do the same for you!

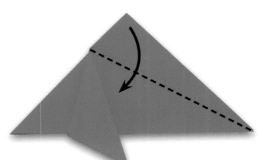

START
WITH A
WATERBOMB
BASE

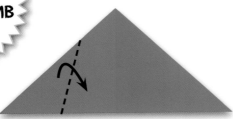

1 Find out how to make a waterbomb base on page 7. Valley fold the upper flap on the left.

2 Valley fold the top right section, as shown.

3 Valley fold the top right flap. This will make the fin on the dolphin's back.

4 Valley fold the left side of the paper across the other folds to make a sharp point. This is the nose.

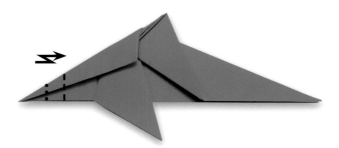

5 Step fold the nose by doing a valley fold and then a mountain fold. This makes it extra pointy!

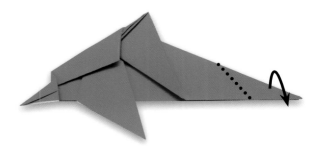

6 Mountain fold the right corner so that it points straight down. This is the tail.

18

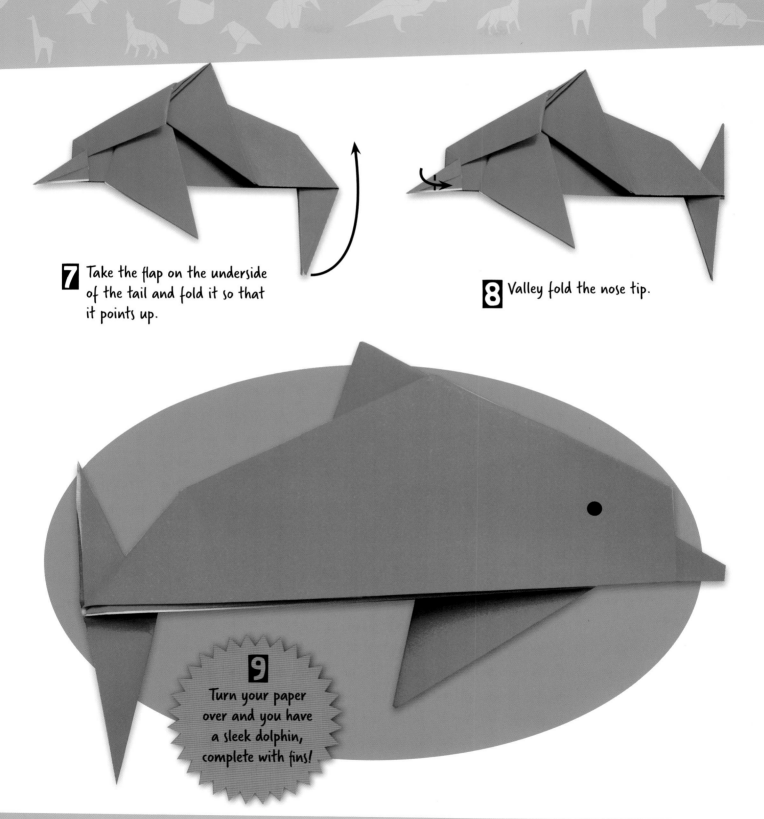

7 Take the flap on the underside of the tail and fold it so that it points up.

8 Valley fold the nose tip.

9 Turn your paper over and you have a sleek dolphin, complete with fins!

Crab

A crab has eight legs, two big claws, and walks sideways!
Check out the claws on this simple origami model version...

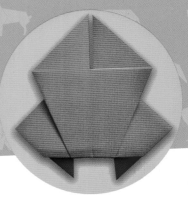

START WITH A WATERBOMB BASE

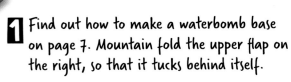

1 Find out how to make a waterbomb base on page 7. Mountain fold the upper flap on the right, so that it tucks behind itself.

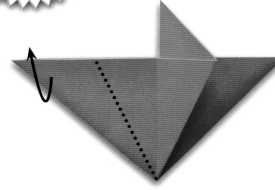

2 Do the same on the other side.

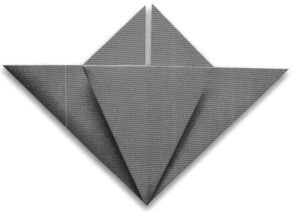

3 You should now have this shape. Make sure the two points at the top line up in the middle.

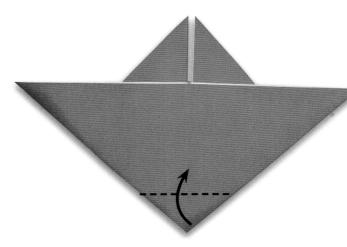

4 Turn the paper over. Valley fold the bottom corner.

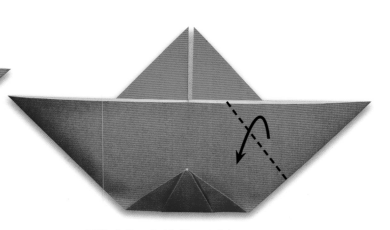

5 Valley fold the right corner.

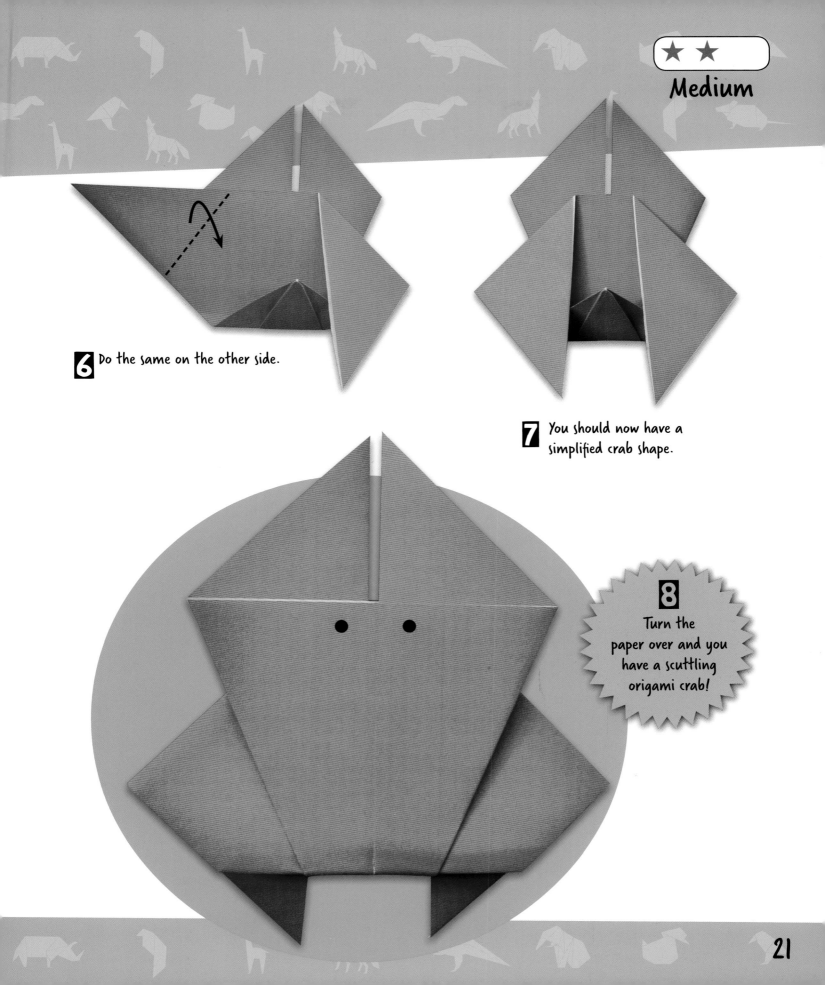

6 Do the same on the other side.

7 You should now have a simplified crab shape.

8 Turn the paper over and you have a scuttling origami crab!

Shark

Sharks glide through the water in search of prey. This dangerous-looking origami shark has its mouth open wide, ready to bite...

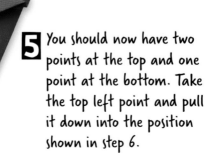

START WITH A BIRD BASE

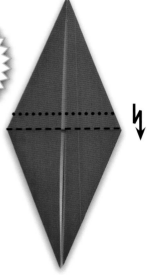

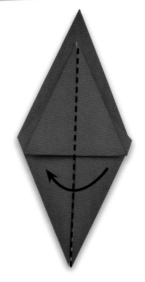

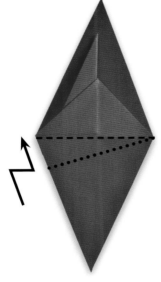

1 Find out how to make a bird base on pages 7-8. The open slit points down. Take the upper, top flap and step fold it as shown.

2 Take the right flap on the top layer and valley fold it along the middle crease.

3 Take the bottom point and valley fold it up along the middle crease, then mountain fold down to make another step fold.

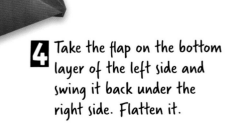

Pull

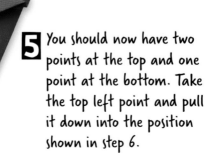

4 Take the flap on the bottom layer of the left side and swing it back under the right side. Flatten it.

5 You should now have two points at the top and one point at the bottom. Take the top left point and pull it down into the position shown in step 6.

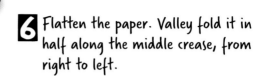

6 Flatten the paper. Valley fold it in half along the middle crease, from right to left.

7 Turn it on its side, as shown. The shark's nose is on the left and its tail is on the right. Mountain fold the right point.

8 You have the beginnings of the tail as above. Unfold and make an outside reverse fold to finish the tail.

9
Now you have a fierce origami shark with a wide-open mouth!

Ray

The ray has a flat body so that it can glide easily through the water. And watch out for that pointy tail, which can give a nasty electric shock!

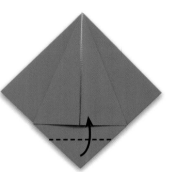

START WITH A SQUARE BASE

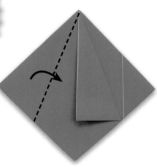

1 Find out how to make a square base on page 6. With the open ends at the top, fold in the upper flap on the top right of the paper.

2 Do the same on the other side.

3 Valley fold the bottom triangle up.

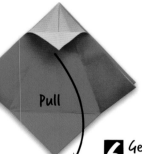

Pull

4 Open out the folds that you made in steps 1–3.

5 The paper should now look like this, opened out.

6 Gently pull the upper flap out and down to open up the middle of the paper.

7 Pull it out until it looks like an open bird's beak.

8 Now flatten the paper so that it looks like this.

9 Valley fold the right side of the paper to meet the middle crease.

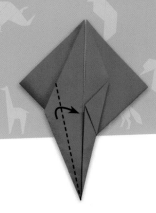

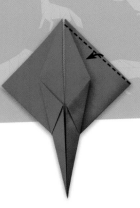

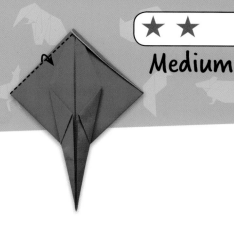

10 Do the same on the other side.

11 Valley fold the right edge of the paper.

12 Do the same on the other side.

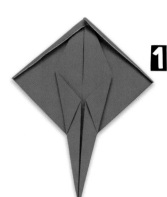

13 The paper should now look like this.

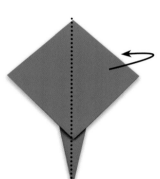

14 Turn the paper over. Mountain fold carefully along the body and tail.

15 Bend and pinch the tail to give it shape. Shape it how you like!

16 Unfold and now you have an origami ray with a dangerous-looking tail!

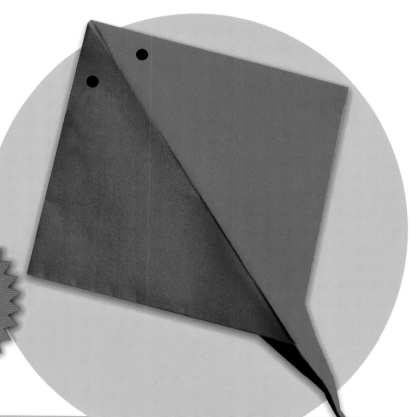

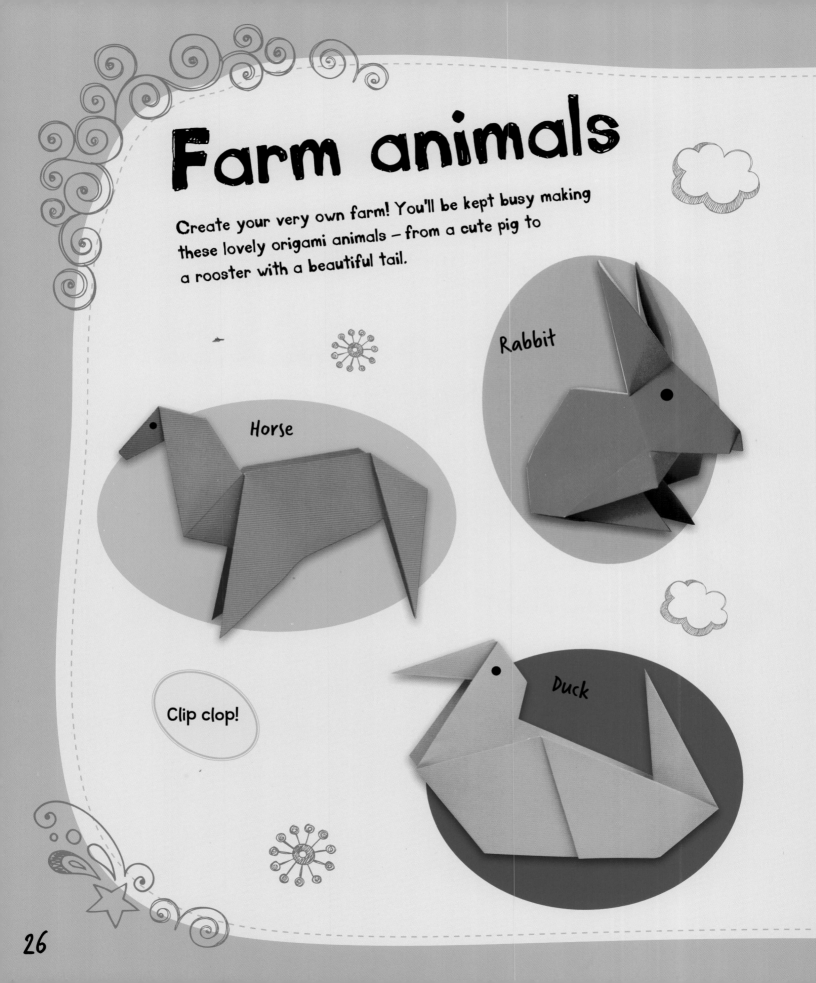

Farm animals

Create your very own farm! You'll be kept busy making these lovely origami animals — from a cute pig to a rooster with a beautiful tail.

Rabbit

Horse

Clip clop!

Duck

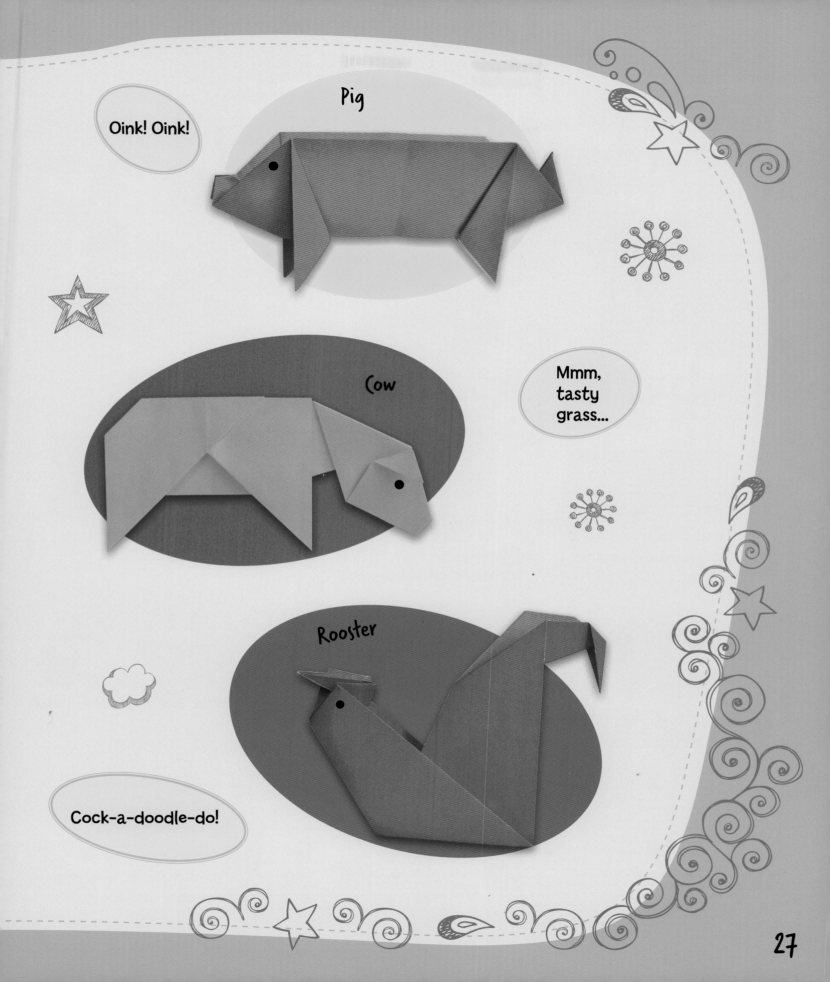

Pig

This cute origami pig stands up on its four pointy feet.
A pig's feet are called trotters.

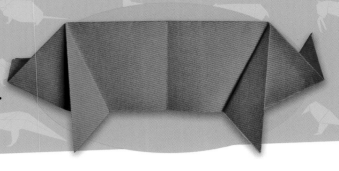

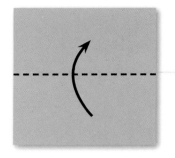

1 Start with a square of paper, white side up. Valley fold the paper in half.

2 Open out the paper. Valley fold the bottom section into the middle crease.

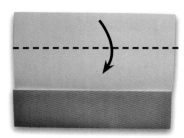

3 Do the same for the top section.

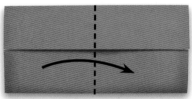

4 Valley fold in half from left to right.

5 The paper should now look like this. Unfold step 4.

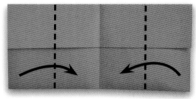

6 Valley fold the outer sections to the middle crease.

7 The paper should now look like this. Unfold step 6.

8 Valley fold the top right corner.

9 Do the same for the other corners.

Open up

10 The paper should now look like this.

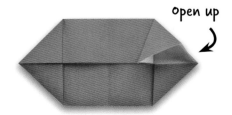

11 Gently open up the top right corner.

12 Flatten it down into a triangle. Do the same for the other corners.

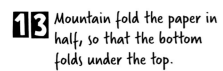
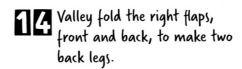

13 Mountain fold the paper in half, so that the bottom folds under the top.

14 Valley fold the right flaps, front and back, to make two back legs.

15 Repeat step 14 to make two front legs.

Close-up of tail

16 Mountain fold the right point.

17 Unfold, then make an inside reverse fold to create the tail. Now mountain fold the left point.

18 Unfold, then make an inside reverse fold to create the nose. Tuck the end inside to make it blunt.

Close-up of nose

19 Now stand your origami pig up on its trotters!

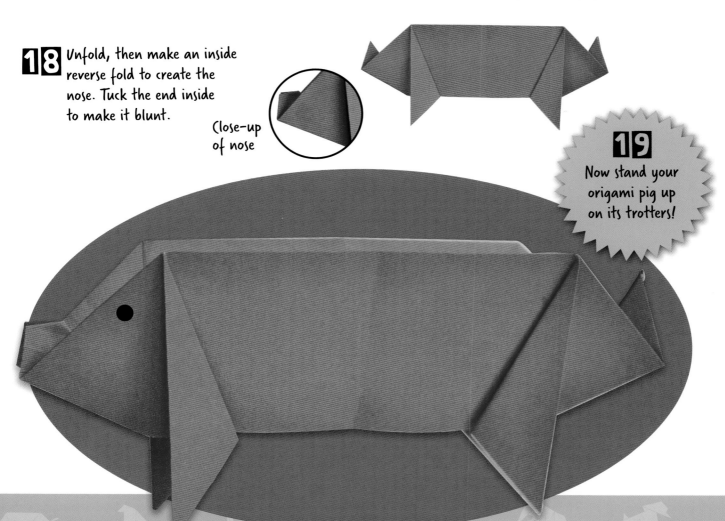

29

Duck

The duck spends a lot of time swimming on lakes and ponds. It has waterproof feathers, so when it dives underwater the top layer of feathers keeps the others dry.

START WITH A KITE BASE

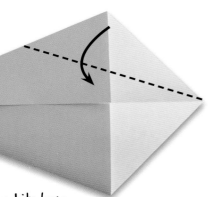

1 Find out how to make a kite base on page 5. Turn it on its side. Valley fold the top right corner to meet the middle crease.

2 Do the same on the other side.

3 Mountain fold the paper in half, so that the bottom folds under the top.

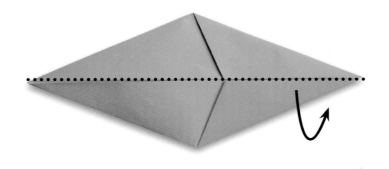

4 Mountain fold the left point.

5 Unfold, then make an inside reverse fold to create the neck.

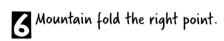

6 Mountain fold the right point.

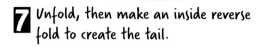

7 Unfold, then make an inside reverse fold to create the tail.

8 Mountain fold the left point.

9 Unfold, then make an inside reverse fold to create the head.

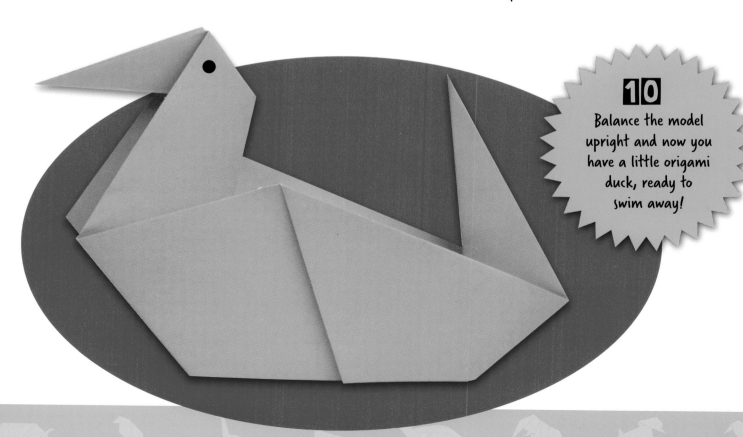

10 Balance the model upright and now you have a little origami duck, ready to swim away!

Rooster

A rooster is a male chicken. He has long, impressive tail feathers, which he uses to show off to the females. Check out this origami rooster's tail.

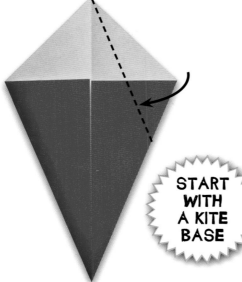

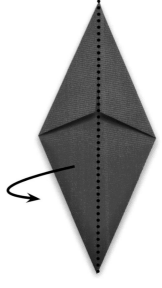

START WITH A KITE BASE

1 Find out how to make a kite base on page 5. Then valley fold the right corner to the middle crease.

2 Do the same on the other side.

3 Mountain fold the paper in half along the middle crease, so that the left side goes behind the right.

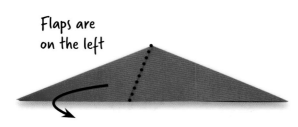

Flaps are on the left

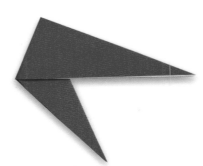

4 Turn the paper on its side. Mountain fold the left point.

5 Unfold, then make an outside reverse fold to create the neck.

6 Mountain fold the right point.

7 Unfold, then make an inside reverse fold to create the tail.

8 Mountain fold the right point.

9 Unfold, then make an outside reverse fold to create the tail feathers.

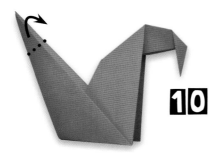

10 Mountain fold the left point.

11 Unfold, then make an inside reverse fold to create the head.

12 Mountain fold the head.

13 Unfold and make another inside reverse fold to create the beak.

14 Now you have an origami rooster with a splendid tail!

33

Horse

The horse is known for its speed and is one of the fastest animals on land. It has four different types of movement – walking, trotting, cantering, and galloping!

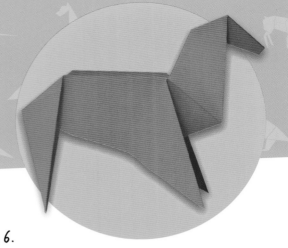

START WITH A FISH BASE

1 Find out how to make a fish base on page 6. Turn it so that the two flaps point to the right. Mountain fold the paper in half, so that the bottom section folds under the top.

2 Mountain fold the left point upward.

3 Unfold, then make an inside reverse fold to create the neck.

4 Mountain fold the top point.

Close-up of head

5 Unfold, then make an inside reverse fold to create the head. Mountain fold the left point.

6 Unfold, then tuck the tip in to make the nose blunt. Valley fold the flaps forward to create the front legs.

7 Mountain fold the right point.

8 Unfold, then make an outside reverse fold to create the back legs.

9 Stand up your origami horse on its strong legs — it's ready to gallop away!

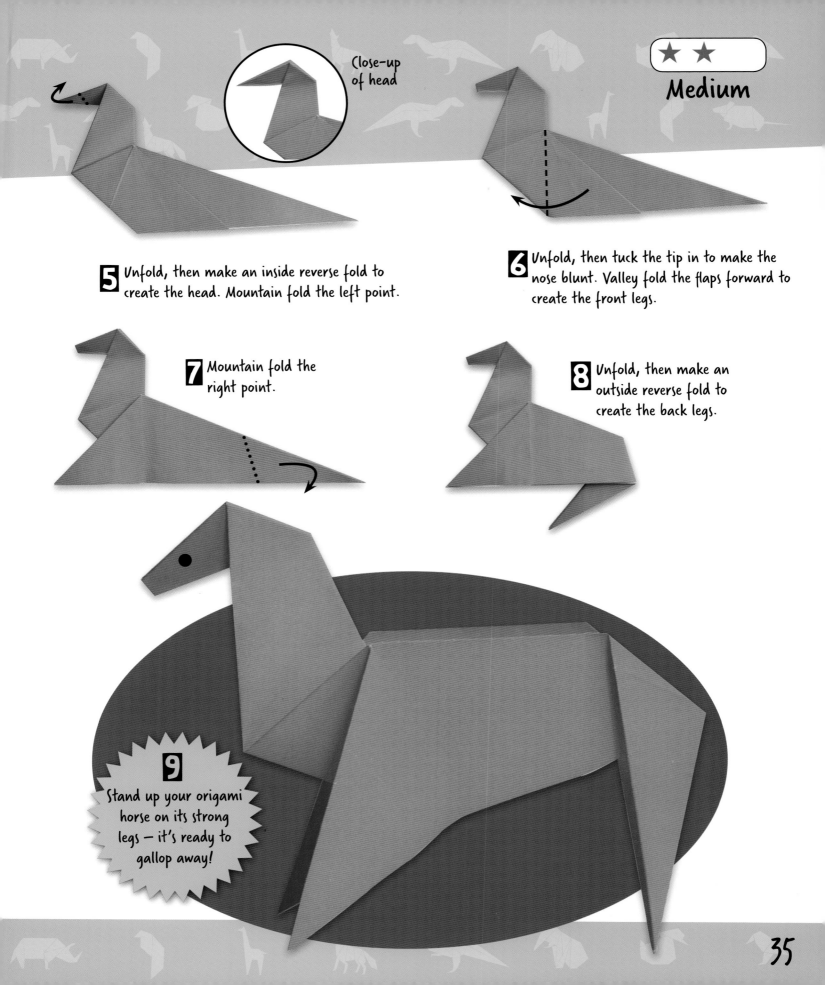

Rabbit

The rabbit has sensitive ears that can be turned in any direction to pick up sounds. Here's how to make an origami version – complete with long ears!

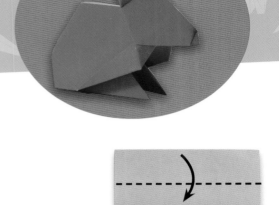

1 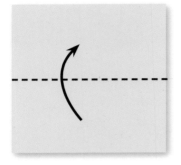 Take a piece of paper and valley fold as shown, then open out again.

2  Valley fold the bottom section up to meet the middle crease.

3  Do the same for the top section.

4  Valley fold the right corner.

5  Valley fold the other corners in the same way.

6 The paper should now look like this.

7  Open out the corner folds.

8 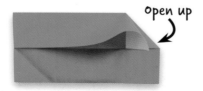 Open up

Gently pull out the top right corner. Tuck the middle fold inside to create a flap.

9  The paper should now look like this.

10 Do the same for the other three corners.

11 Turn the paper over.

12 Turn back the right flap and flatten down.

13 Repeat steps 11 and 12 for the left side.

14 Turn the paper over. Valley fold the top left corner.

15 Do the same on the bottom left.

16 Valley fold the left flaps, so that the left point springs into place. These are the rabbit's ears.

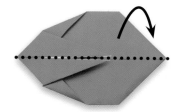

17 Mountain fold along the middle crease, so that the top folds behind.

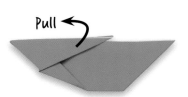

Pull

18 Gently pull the ears up into position.

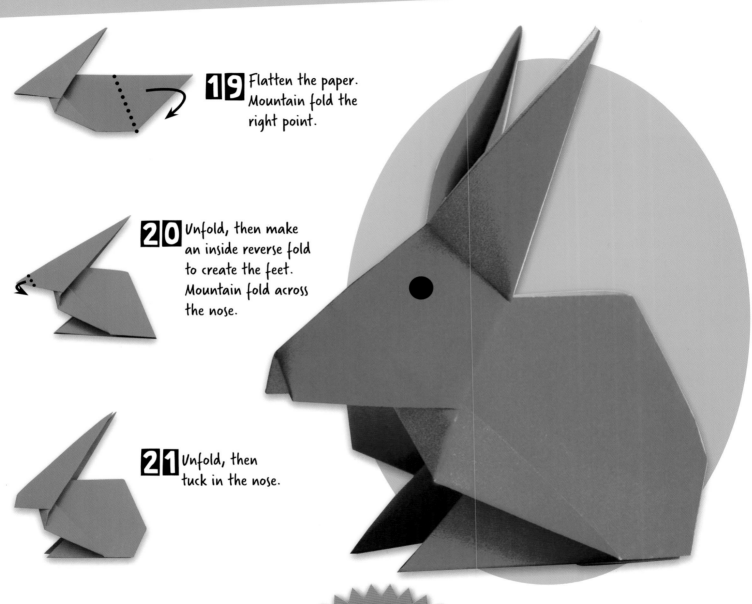

19 Flatten the paper. Mountain fold the right point.

20 Unfold, then make an inside reverse fold to create the feet. Mountain fold across the nose.

21 Unfold, then tuck in the nose.

22 Gently puff out the long ears to give them their shape — and you have your origami rabbit!

Cow

In order to produce all the milk we need, cows need to eat a lot of grass and drink plenty of water every day.

MAKE THE HEAD

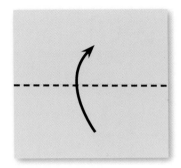

1 Start with the paper white side up. Valley fold the paper in half, then open it again.

2 Valley fold the bottom section up to meet the middle crease.

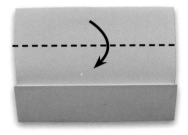

3 Do the same for the top section.

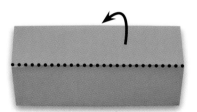

4 Mountain fold the top half back under the bottom half.

5 Valley fold the right corner flap up.

6 Gently open up the top corner.

7 You should see a triangle shape begin to form.

8 Flatten down the paper.

9 Turn the paper over and repeat steps 5 through to 8. From above, the paper looks like this.

Cow... continued

MAKE THE BODY

10 Turn the paper back over. Mountain fold the right tip.

Close-up of nose

11 Unfold, then tuck the tip back into the crease with an inside reverse fold to create the nose.

12 Valley fold the right corner of the flap to create ears on both sides. Mountain fold the left side.

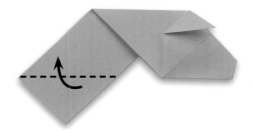

13 Valley fold the bottom corner to make a triangle.

14 The paper should now look like this.

15 Unfold the triangle, then make an inside reverse fold for slotting onto the body.

START WITH A WATERBOMB BASE

1 Find out how to make a waterbomb base on page 7. Valley fold the left tip.

Open here

2 Gently open the base from the right.

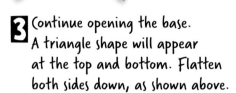

3 Continue opening the base. A triangle shape will appear at the top and bottom. Flatten both sides down, as shown above.

4 Valley fold the paper in half from top to bottom.

5 Turn the paper over. Mountain fold the left corner. Unfold, then make an inside reverse fold to shape the cow's body.

PUT THE COW TOGETHER

1 Slot the head into the body so that it grips firmly.

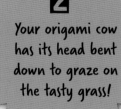

2 Your origami cow has its head bent down to graze on the tasty grass!

Wild animals

There's a huge variety of amazing creatures out there! Create your own wild world with this bunch of exciting origami animals, from a wily fox to a jumping frog!

Fox

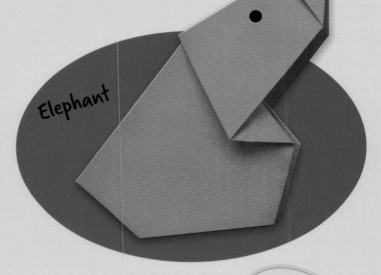

Elephant

What a long trunk!

Panda

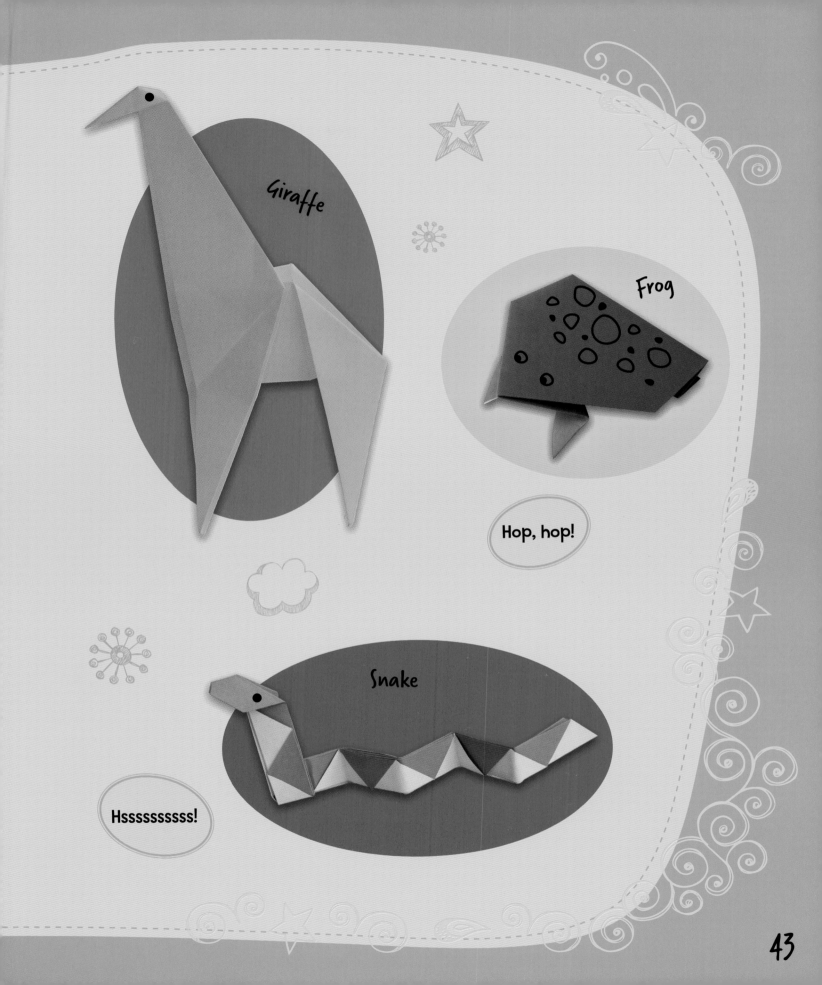

Fox

In many traditional stories, the fox is a symbol of trickery and cunning. You'll find that making this origami fox isn't too tricky, though!

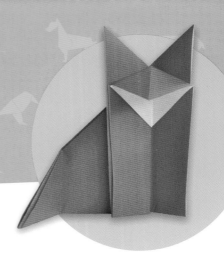

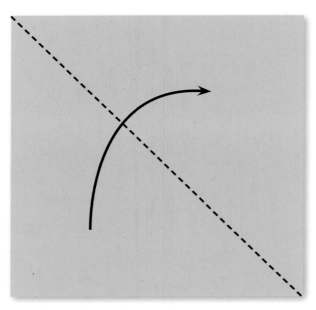

1 Start with a square of paper, white side up. Valley fold in half diagonally.

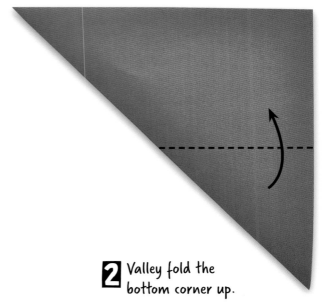

2 Valley fold the bottom corner up.

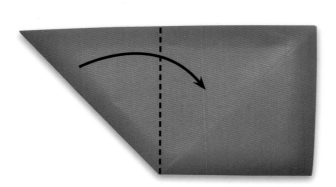

3 Now valley fold the left corner in to meet it.

4 Mountain fold the left section behind the right section.

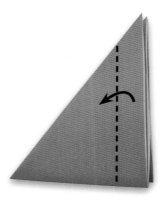

5 Valley fold the right section.

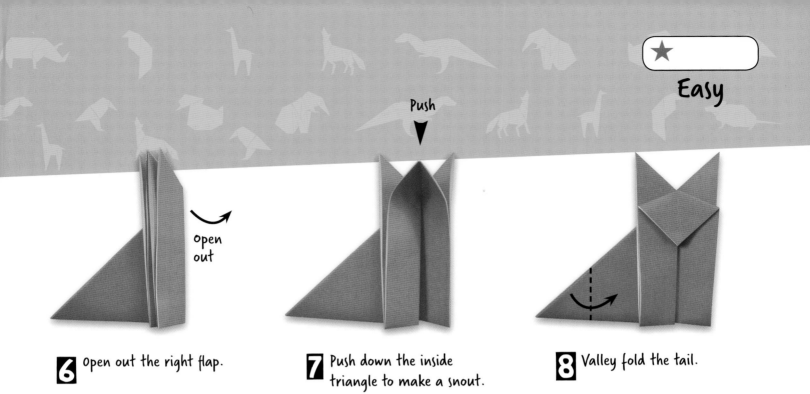
Push

6 Open out the right flap.

open out

7 Push down the inside triangle to make a snout.

8 Valley fold the tail.

9 Open up the mouth. Now you have your cunning, but cute, origami fox!

Snake

Snakes don't have legs, so instead they use their strong muscles to move themselves along the ground in a wavy motion.

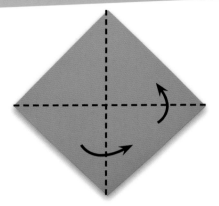

1 Start with your paper like this. Make two diagonal valley folds.

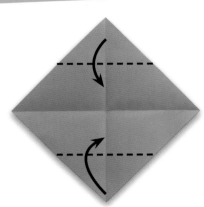

2 Valley fold the top and bottom corners to meet in the middle.

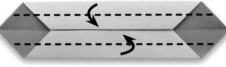

3 Valley fold the top and bottom sections to meet in the middle.

4 Repeat step 3.

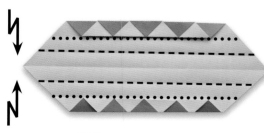

5 The paper should now look like this.

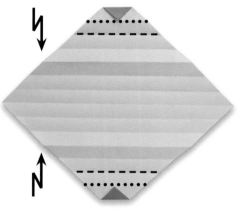

6 Unfold and turn the paper over. Then start to make a series of step folds inward from both ends.

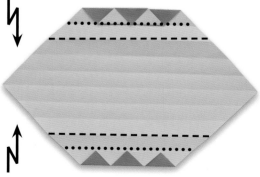

7 Continue to step fold. A pattern like this should appear.

8 Repeat step 7.

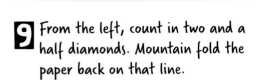

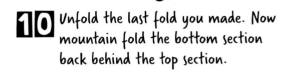

9 From the left, count in two and a half diamonds. Mountain fold the paper back on that line.

10 Unfold the last fold you made. Now mountain fold the bottom section back behind the top section.

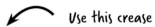

Use this crease

11 Using the crease on the left that you made in step 9, make an outside reverse fold.

12 Mountain fold the top left corner.

13 Unfold, then make an outside reverse fold to create the snake's head.

14 Make alternate mountain and valley folds along the body.

15 Arrange the model like this. Now you have a zigzagging origami snake!

Panda

The panda is well-known for its striking black-and-white markings. Origami paper that is dark on one side and white on the other works really well for this model.

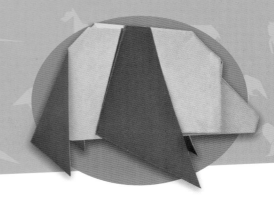

START WITH A WATERBOMB BASE

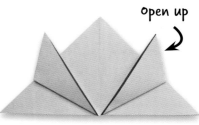

1 Find out how to make a waterbomb base on page 7. Make sure the white side is facing out. Valley fold the right flap.

2 Do the same on the other side.

3 Gently open up the flap on the right.

Open up

4 Make an outside reverse fold on this flap. Then do the same on the other side.

5 Valley fold the right tip of the bottom point.

6 Do the same on the other side.

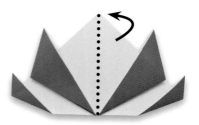

Open up

7 Gently open up the bottom right flap.

8 Make an outside reverse fold. Then do the same on the other side.

9 Mountain fold the paper in half along the middle crease.

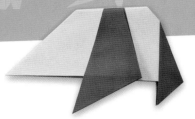

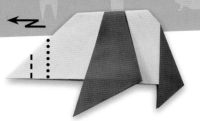

10 Turn the paper sideways, so that you now have the shape of the panda's body and legs. Mountain fold the top corner.

11 Unfold, then make an inside reverse fold to create the panda's back, as shown.

12 Step fold to make the panda's face.

13 Mountain fold the left point.

14 Unfold, then tuck the paper in to give the panda a blunt nose.

15 Open the model out and stand it up to make a perfect origami panda!

Elephant

An elephant's trunk is strong and sensitive. It's used for grasping food and sucking up water. Here's how to make an origami elephant with an impressive trunk!

START WITH A KITE BASE

1 Find out how to make a kite base on page 5. Turn it upside down and turn the paper over.

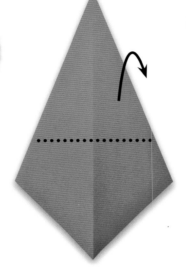

2 Mountain fold the paper in half.

3 The paper should now look like this.

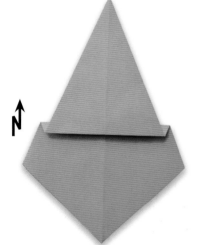

4 Open the paper out and then make a valley fold, to create a step fold as shown. Then turn the paper over.

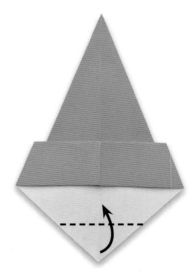

5 Valley fold the bottom tip to meet the edge of the paper above.

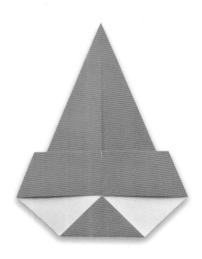

6 The paper should now look like this.

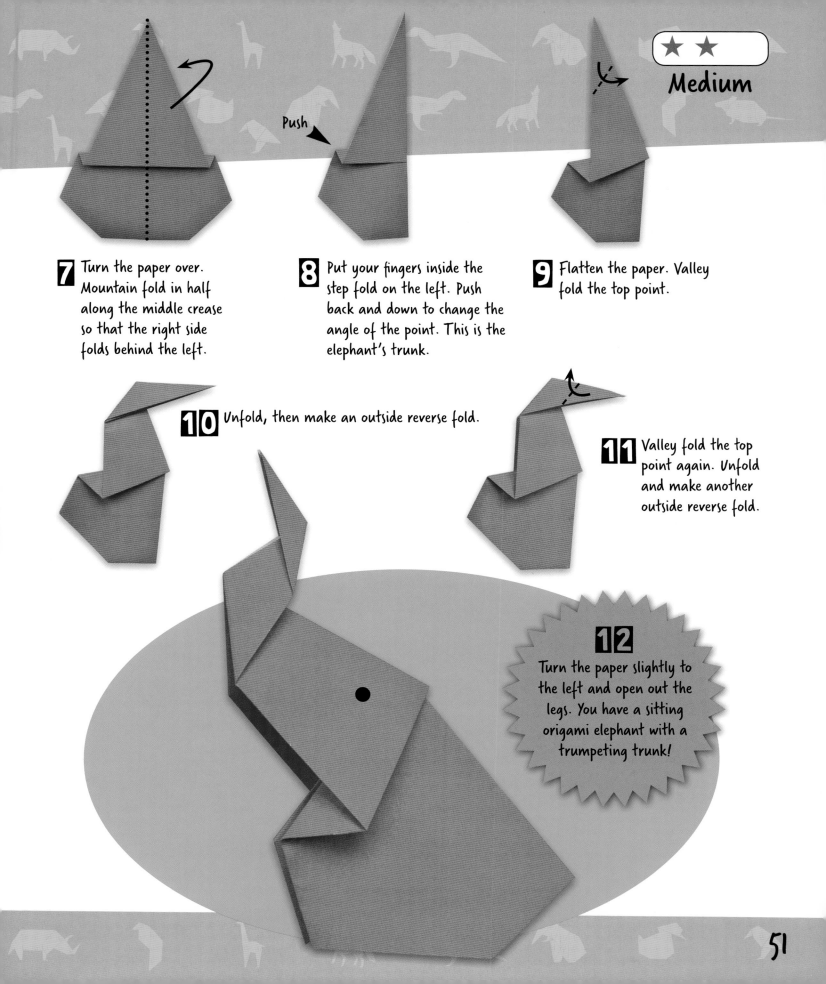

Push

7 Turn the paper over. Mountain fold in half along the middle crease so that the right side folds behind the left.

8 Put your fingers inside the step fold on the left. Push back and down to change the angle of the point. This is the elephant's trunk.

9 Flatten the paper. Valley fold the top point.

10 Unfold, then make an outside reverse fold.

11 Valley fold the top point again. Unfold and make another outside reverse fold.

12 Turn the paper slightly to the left and open out the legs. You have a sitting origami elephant with a trumpeting trunk!

51

Giraffe

The giraffe has the longest neck of any animal on Earth. It uses its neck to reach juicy leaves at the tops of trees.

START WITH A BIRD BASE

1 Find out how to make a bird base on pages 7–8. Position it so that the flaps with the open slit are on the left.

2 Take the right flap on the bottom layer and swing it around behind to the left, so that the two flaps are now in the middle as shown.

3 Take the left and right points, one in each hand, and gently pull the base open, so that it looks like this.

Pull   Pull

4 Continue pulling gently until the middle section starts to open like a bird's beak.

5 Open the paper slightly and make a mountain fold from the middle crease.

6 Close the paper again and press the left and right points together to make a star.

7 Bring the bottom point up to meet the top point. Flatten the paper.

8 Turn the paper over, so that the point is now facing down.

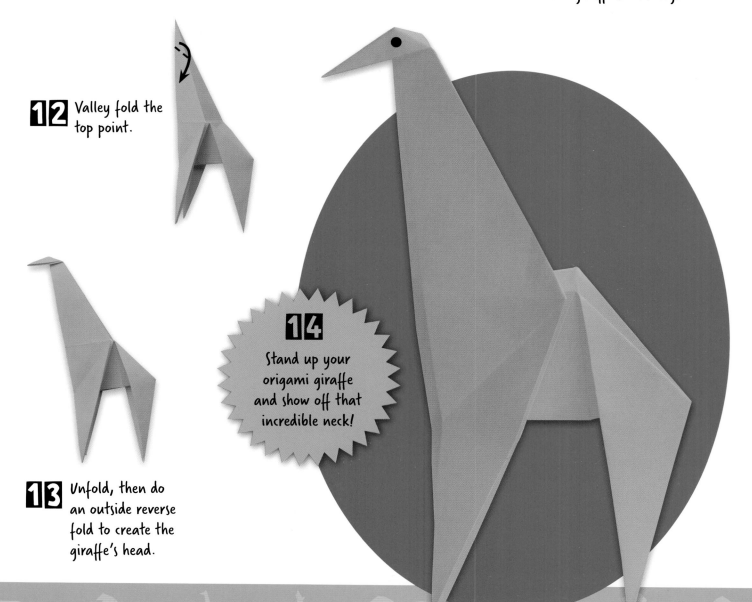

Push

9 Push the left point up and back so that the back flap goes behind, and the front flap swings around in front.

10 Flatten the paper. Valley fold the right point.

11 Unfold, then make an outside reverse fold to create the giraffe's back legs.

12 Valley fold the top point.

14
Stand up your origami giraffe and show off that incredible neck!

13 Unfold, then do an outside reverse fold to create the giraffe's head.

Frog

Frogs move by jumping on their strong back legs. Here's how to make an origami frog that can spring into action!

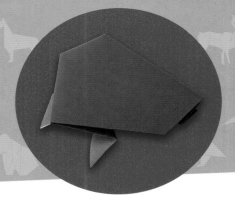

1 Start with your paper white side up. Valley fold the paper in half from left to right.

2 Valley fold the top left and right sides diagonally, crease well, and then unfold.

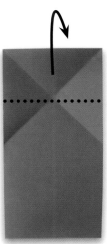

3 Mountain fold the top section in half at the point where the diagonal lines cross. Crease and then unfold.

4 Collapse the top section by pushing in the sides.

5 Your model should look like this. Push the top edge down to flatten it.

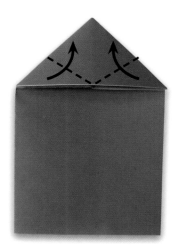

6 Valley fold the left and right sides of the top triangle to create your frog's front legs.

7 Valley fold the bottom square in half.

8 Valley fold the top flap down.

9 Your model should now look like this. Turn your model over.

10 Your model should look like this. Use a pen to add features to your frog.

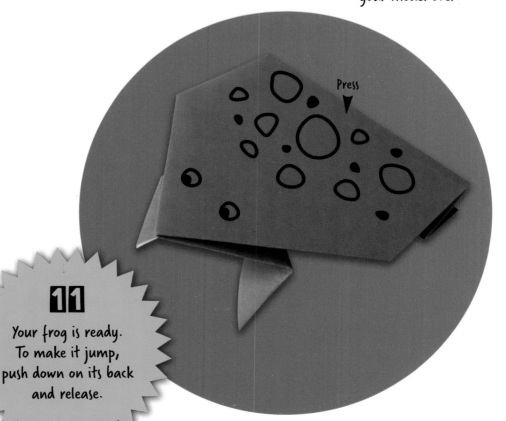

Press

11

Your frog is ready. To make it jump, push down on its back and release.

Pets

Is there a pet that you've always wanted to own? Why not make yourself an origami version? There's plenty to choose from here, from a cool cat to a swimming turtle!

Goldfish

Squeak, squeak!

Mouse

Cat

Meow!

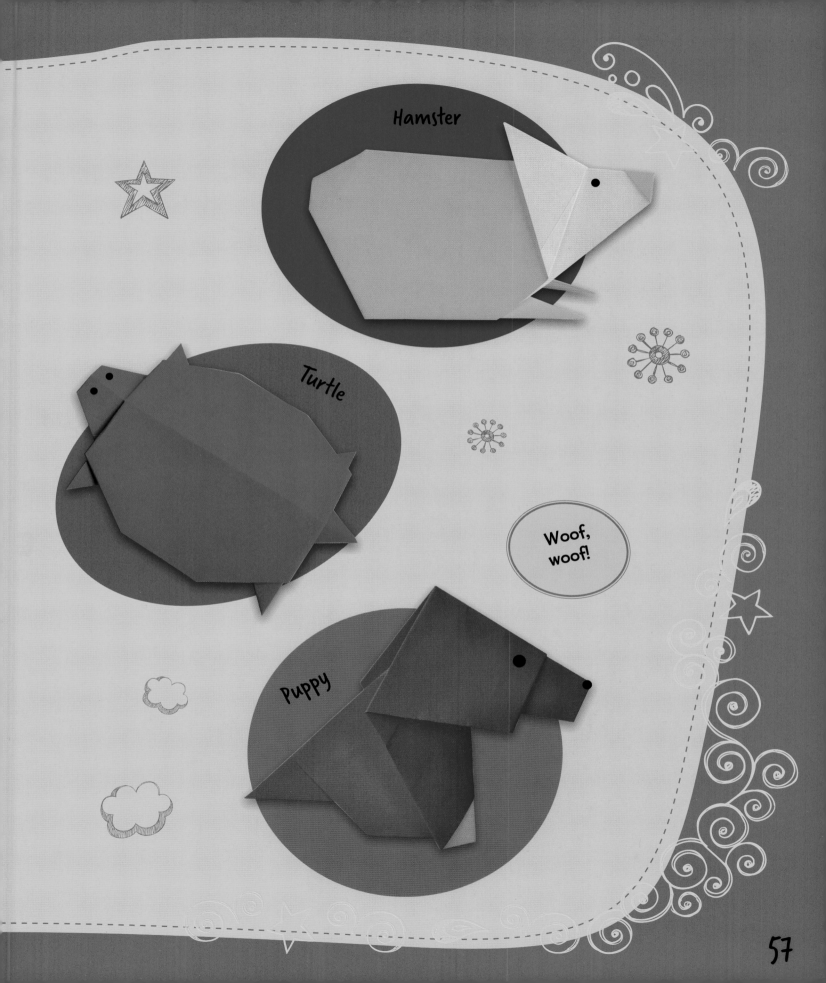

Hamster

The hamster carries food in special pouches in its cheeks. When the pouches are full, the hamster's face can look enormous!

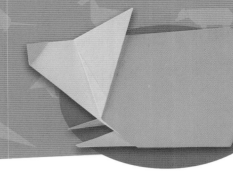

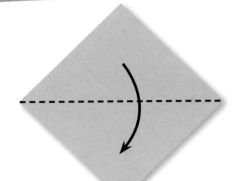

1 Start with a square of paper in this position, white side up. Valley fold it in half diagonally.

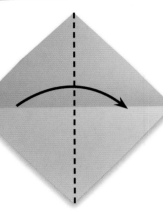

2 Open the paper and valley fold it in half diagonally the other way.

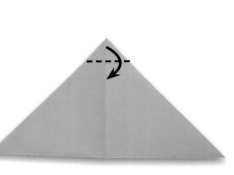

3 Turn the paper so that the point is upward, as shown. Valley fold the tip of the top flap.

4 Valley fold the tip of the flap underneath.

5 The paper should now look like this. Turn the paper over.

6 Valley fold the right corner to make a flap.

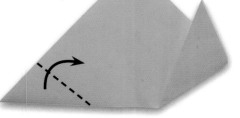

7 Do the same on the other side.

58

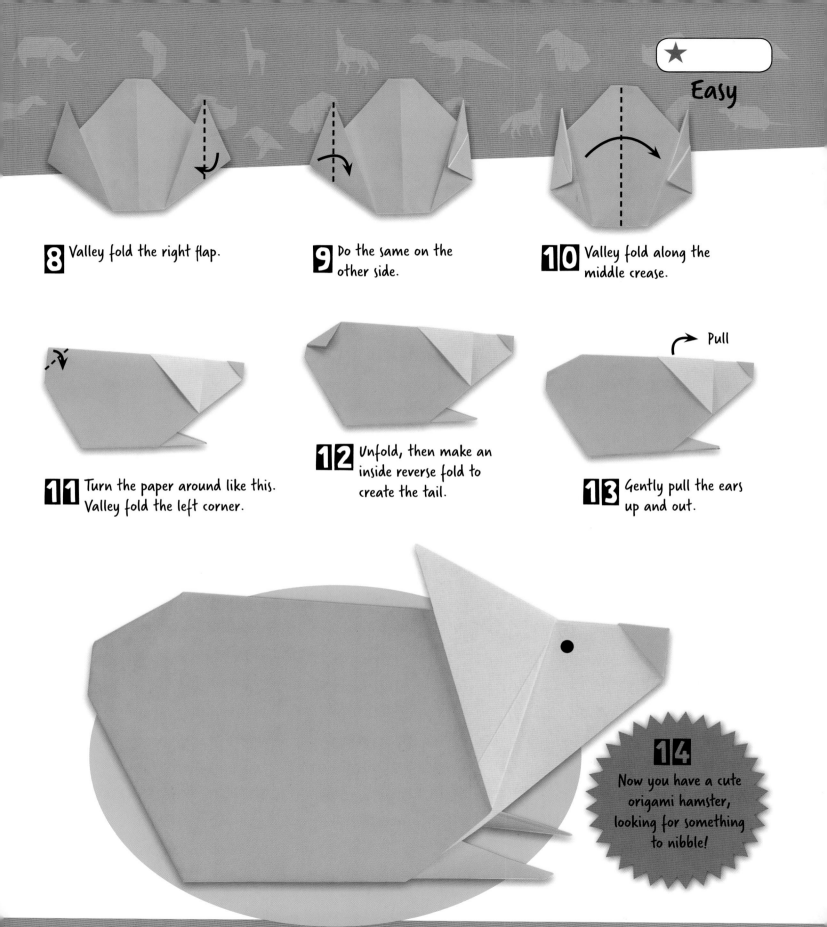

8 Valley fold the right flap.

9 Do the same on the other side.

10 Valley fold along the middle crease.

11 Turn the paper around like this. Valley fold the left corner.

12 Unfold, then make an inside reverse fold to create the tail.

Pull

13 Gently pull the ears up and out.

14 Now you have a cute origami hamster, looking for something to nibble!

Puppy

Puppies are bouncy and playful, but they have to be trained to do what they're told! Here's a fun origami puppy, just for you.

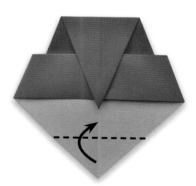

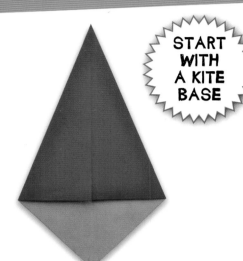

START WITH A KITE BASE

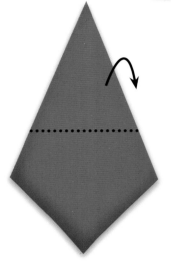

1 Find out how to make a kite base on page 5. Turn it upside down. Turn the paper over.

2 Mountain fold it in half so that the top section goes behind the bottom section.

3 The paper should now look like this. Unfold.

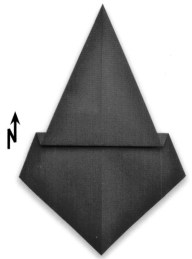

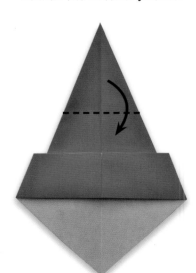

4 Make a valley fold just beneath the crease to make a step fold. Turn the paper over.

5 Valley fold the top point.

6 Valley fold the bottom point up to meet the tip of the top section.

7 Valley fold the top section up and the bottom section down.

8 Fold the top tip down in a valley fold.

9 Valley fold the paper in half along the middle crease from right to left.

Push

10 Turn the paper around, as shown here. Valley fold and crease well. Unfold, then gently push down and back on the puppy's nose.

11 As you push, the flaps pop back into place, revealing the puppy's white feet.

12 Stand up your origami model and you have a perfectly cute, puppy playmate!

Goldfish

Although they're called goldfish, these fish actually come in many varieties, including red, orange, yellow, white, black, and brown. Make yours a bright one!

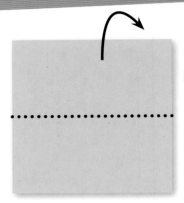

1 Start with a square of paper, white side up. Mountain fold it in half, taking the top section back behind the bottom section.

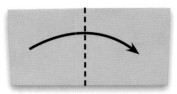

2 Valley fold it in half from left to right.

3 The paper should now look like this.

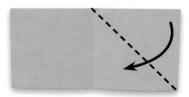

4 Open the paper out. Valley fold the right corner.

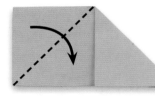

5 Do the same on the other side.

6 The paper should now look like this.

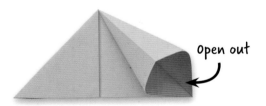

Open out

7 Gently open out the right corner.

8 Flatten the paper to make a kite shape, as shown.

9 Repeat steps 7 and 8 on the other side.

10 Turn the paper over. Valley fold the right corner.

11 Do the same on the other side.

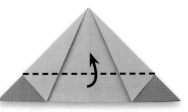

12 Valley fold the upper flap.

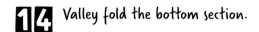

13 The paper should now look like this. Turn it over.

14 Valley fold the bottom section.

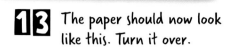

15 Valley fold the right upper flap.

16 Do the same on the other side.

17 Mountain fold the right and left corners at the back.

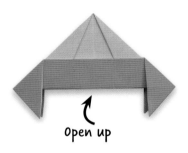

Open up

18 The paper should now look like this. Start to open the bottom out.

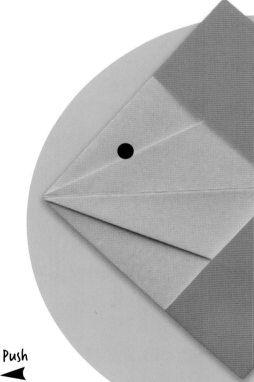

Push   Push

19 Push the left and right sides together until they snap shut.

20

Turn the model sideways, pull out the tail fins, and you have a fabulous origami goldfish!

Mouse

The mouse has an excellent sense of smell and investigates its surroundings with a long, pointy nose – just like this origami version!

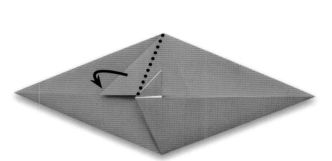

START WITH A FISH BASE

1 Find out how to make a fish base on page 6. Turn it so that the flaps are pointing to the left. Mountain fold the bottom flap and tuck it under itself.

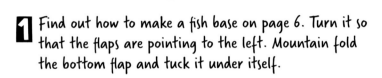

2 Mountain fold the top flap and tuck it under the bottom flap.

3 Mountain fold the left point.

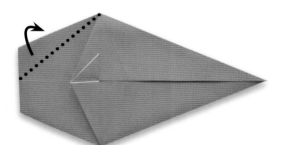

4 Mountain fold the top left corner.

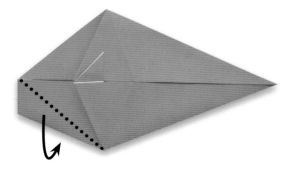

5 Do the same on the other side.

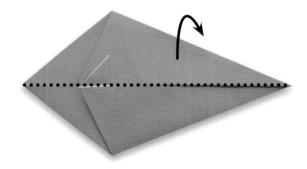

6 Mountain fold in half, so that the top section folds down behind the bottom section.

7 Valley fold the front flap. Then do the same to the back flap to create the ears.

8 Mountain fold the right point and then valley fold to make a step fold.

9 Unfold and do an inside reverse fold to make the tail point down, as shown. Then do a second inside reverse fold to tuck the tail back up.

10 Mountain fold the right edge of the front flap of the tail to tuck it in and make it narrow. Do the same for the back flap.

11 Open out the ears and pull the tail down gently.

Pull

12 You now have an inquisitive origami mouse, complete with a pointy nose and tail!

Turtle

The turtle spends a lot of time in water. It has powerful flippers to help it swim. It also has a hard, rounded shell to protect it from predators.

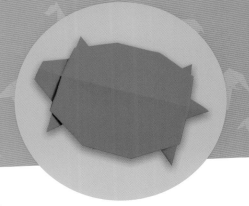

1 Start with your paper white side up. Valley fold it in half and open it out.

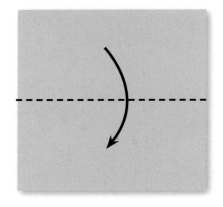

2 Valley fold the bottom section up to the middle crease.

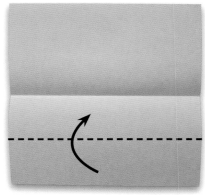

3 Do the same for the top section.

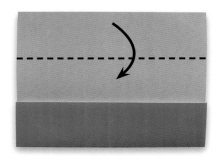

4 Valley fold the right corner.

5 Do the same on the other side.

6 The paper should now look like this.

7 Gently open out the top corner.

Open out

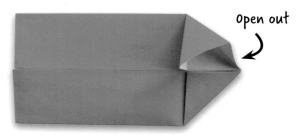

8 Flatten the paper to make a triangle shape as shown.

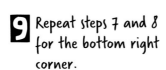

9 Repeat steps 7 and 8 for the bottom right corner.

10 Repeat steps 4 to 9 for the left corners.

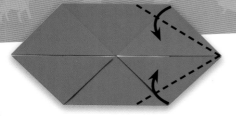

11 Valley fold the top and bottom right corners.

12 Repeat step 11 for the left corners.

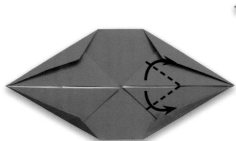

13 Valley fold the flaps on the right to create the turtle's feet.

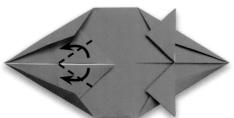

14 Do the same on the other side.

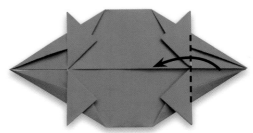

15 Valley fold the right point into the body.

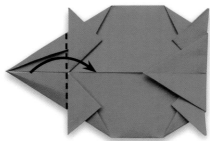

16 Do the same on the other side.

17 Valley fold the right point back.

Turtle... continued

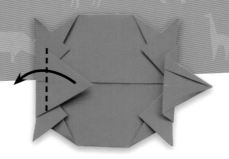

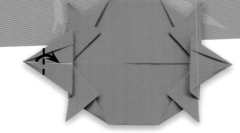

18 Do the same on the other side.

19 Valley fold the left tip. This is the turtle's nose.

20 Turn the paper over. Bend it slightly along the middle crease.

21 Now stand your origami turtle up on its claws. It's ready for a dip in the water!

Cat

Cats have lived with people as pets for thousands of years. The cat makes a good companion, since it's friendly and loves to sit on laps!

MAKE THE HEAD

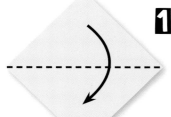

1 Begin with a square of paper white side up, and positioned like this. Valley fold it in half diagonally.

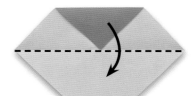

2 Open it out, then valley fold the top tip to meet the middle crease.

3 Valley fold the top section down along the middle crease.

4 Valley fold the right corner down.

5 Do the same on the other side.

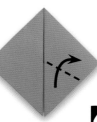

6 Valley fold the bottom right corner up.

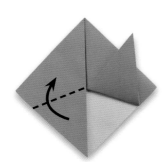

7 Do the same on the other side. These are the cat's ears.

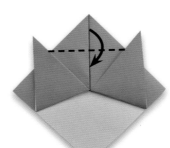

8 Valley fold the top triangle between the ears.

9 The paper should now look like this.

69

Cat... continued

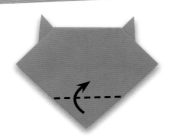

10 Turn the paper over. Valley fold the bottom corner.

11 Valley fold the tip of the bottom triangle to create the cat's nose.

12 You now have the cat's head.

MAKE THE BODY

> **START WITH A KITE BASE**

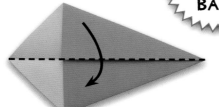

1 Find out how to make a kite base on page 5. Turn it on its side, as shown. Valley fold in half.

2 Valley fold the right point.

3 Valley fold the right corner.

4 The paper should now look like this.

5 Open up the folds you made in steps 2 and 3.

Open out

6 Gently lift the right corner and open it out.

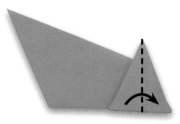

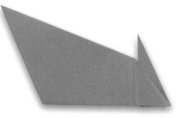

7 Flatten the paper down into a kite shape as shown. Valley fold the bottom triangle.

8 Valley fold the left flap of the triangle over to the right to create the cat's tail.

9 You now have the cat's body, as shown above.

PUT THE CAT TOGETHER

1 Balance the head on the top point of the cat's body.

2 Now fold out the back legs — and you have an origami cat to make friends with!

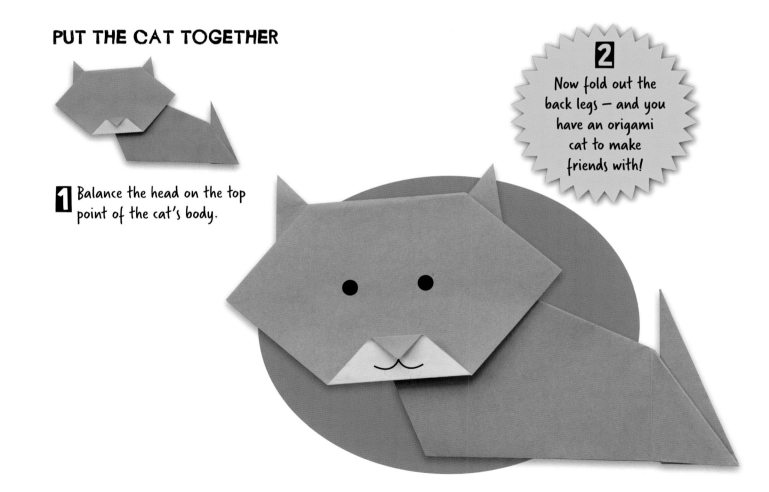

Birds

Find out how to make a variety of beautiful birds in this chapter. Your origami models will look like they are ready to take flight!

Pelican

Songbird

Beautiful singing!

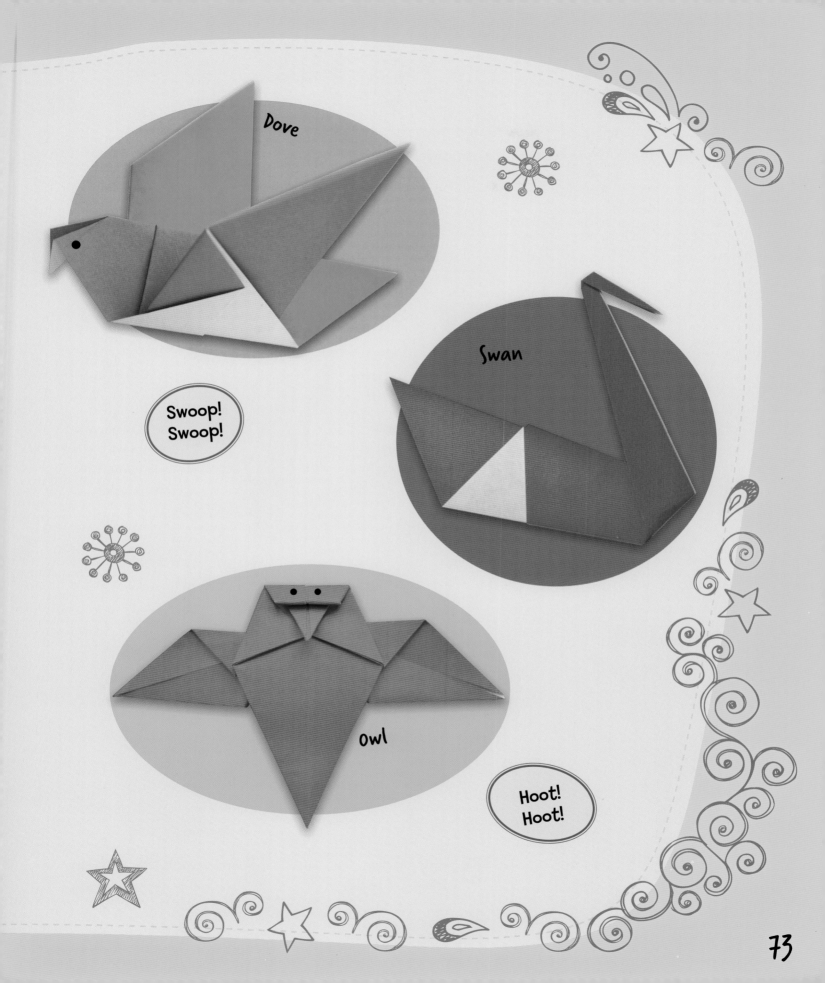

Swan

There are few more elegant sights than a graceful swan gliding across a lake. Here's how to make one.

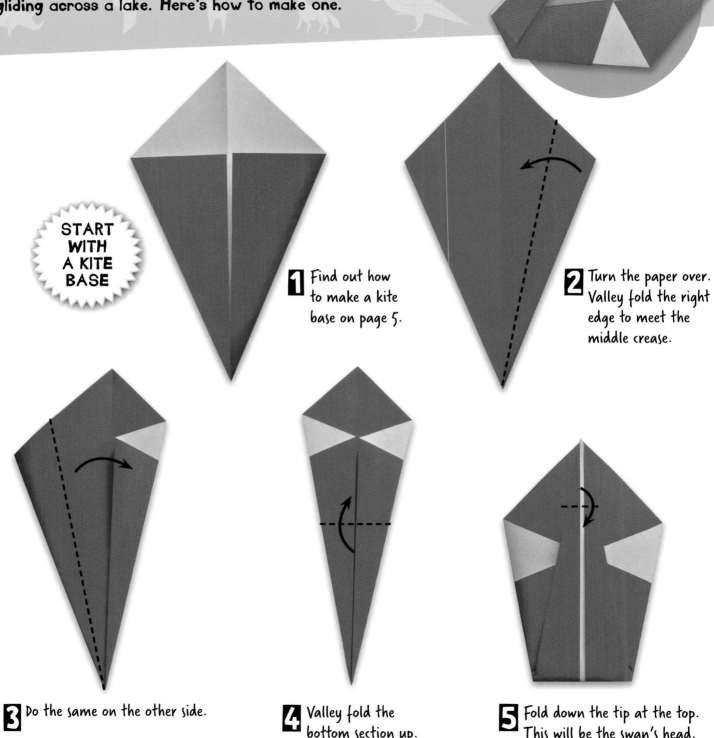

START WITH A KITE BASE

1 Find out how to make a kite base on page 5.

2 Turn the paper over. Valley fold the right edge to meet the middle crease.

3 Do the same on the other side.

4 Valley fold the bottom section up.

5 Fold down the tip at the top. This will be the swan's head.

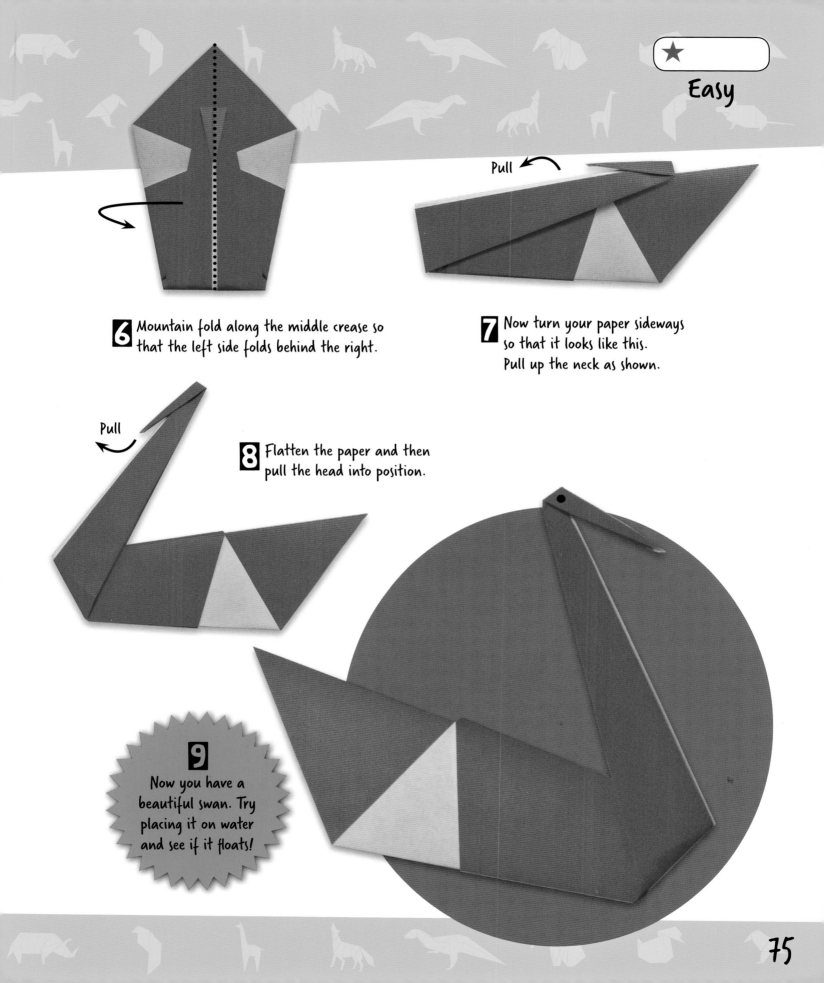

6 Mountain fold along the middle crease so that the left side folds behind the right.

7 Now turn your paper sideways so that it looks like this. Pull up the neck as shown.

Pull

8 Flatten the paper and then pull the head into position.

Pull

9 Now you have a beautiful swan. Try placing it on water and see if it floats!

Pelican

The pelican has an extremely long beak which it uses to scoop up fish and other small creatures to eat. Gulp!

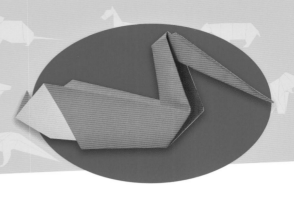

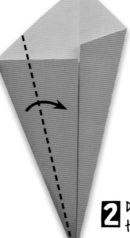

START WITH A KITE BASE

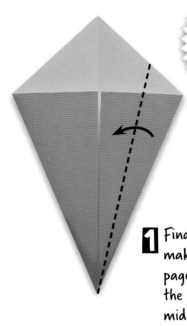

1 Find out how to make a kite base on page 5. Valley fold the right edge to the middle crease.

2 Do the same on the other side.

3 The paper should now look like this.

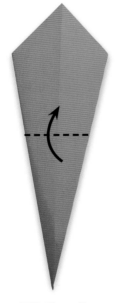

4 Turn the paper over and valley fold the bottom up.

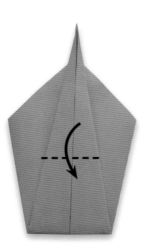

5 Fold the top tip down.

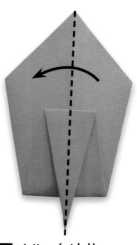

6 Valley fold the paper in half from right to left.

7 Turn the paper sideways, so that the tip points out to the left as shown.

8 Gently pull the neck of the pelican from inside so that it sits upright. Mountain fold the tail.

9 Unfold, then make an inside reverse fold to create the tail.

10 You now have a perfectly poised pelican ready to go and catch some fish with that huge beak!

Dove

The dove is traditionally used as a symbol of peace and love. Make your own peace symbol with this origami version!

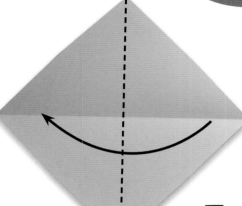

1 Start with a square of paper in this position, white side up. Valley fold it as shown.

2 Open the paper out and valley fold it again.

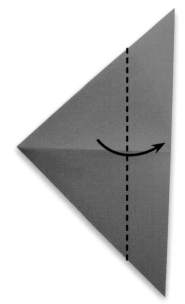

3 Valley fold the left point from left to right.

4 Valley fold the right point from right to left.

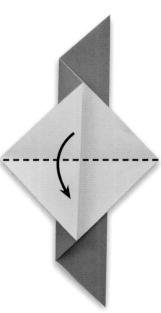

5 Open the top flap and fold back the right corner. Valley fold on the middle crease.

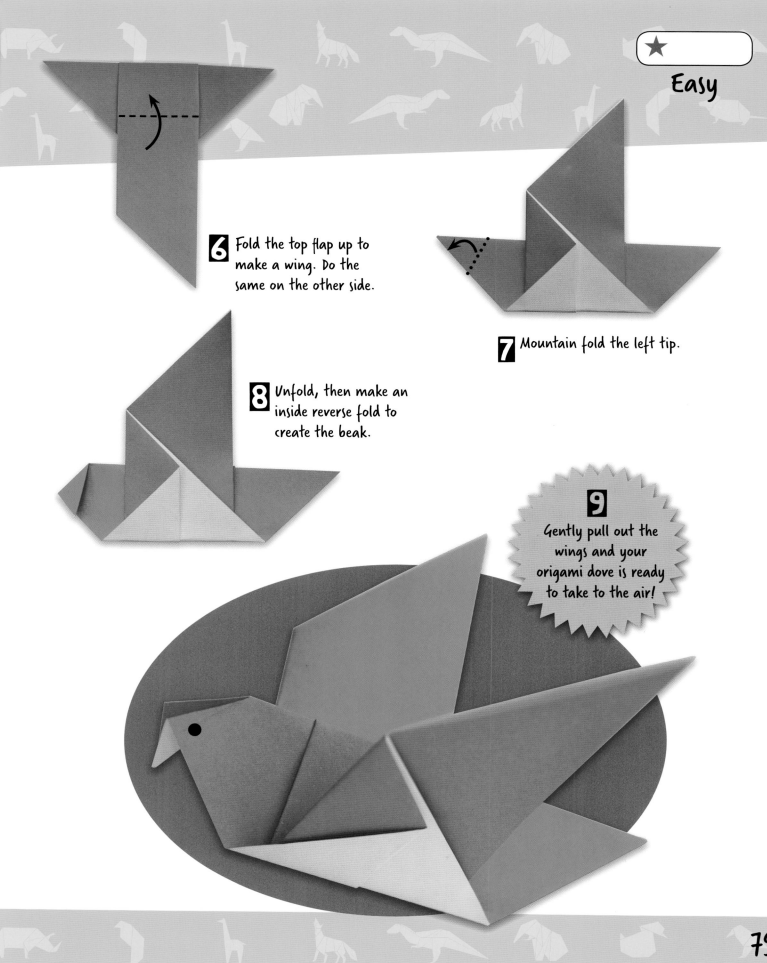

6 Fold the top flap up to make a wing. Do the same on the other side.

7 Mountain fold the left tip.

8 Unfold, then make an inside reverse fold to create the beak.

9 Gently pull out the wings and your origami dove is ready to take to the air!

Songbird

Many different types of small birds can be found in gardens and parks. Here's how to make the origami kind!

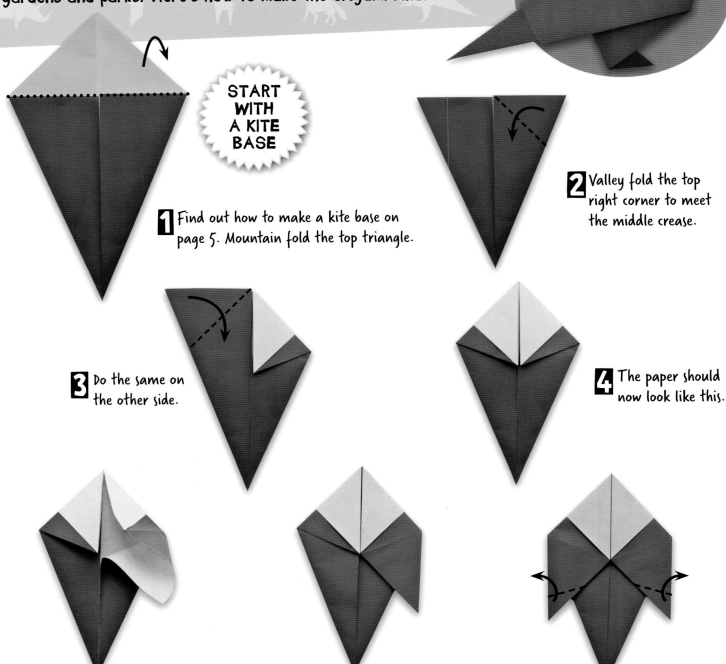

START WITH A KITE BASE

1 Find out how to make a kite base on page 5. Mountain fold the top triangle.

2 Valley fold the top right corner to meet the middle crease.

3 Do the same on the other side.

4 The paper should now look like this.

5 Gently open out the right corner.

6 Flatten the paper to make this shape. Repeat on the other side.

7 Valley fold both tips. These will become the bird's feet.

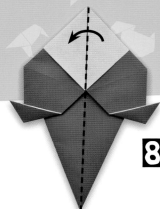

8 Valley fold the paper in half along the middle crease, from right to left.

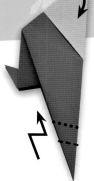

9 Step fold the lower point. Unfold, then tuck the tail in and then out again along the fold lines. Valley fold the top point.

10 Turn the paper sideways. Unfold, then make an inside reverse fold to create the head.

11 This is what your songbird should look like from above.

12 Stand your model up on its feet. Your origami bird now looks ready to burst into song!

Owl

The owl is often used as a symbol of wisdom and knowledge. Your origami owl looks powerful and alert as it opens its wings wide.

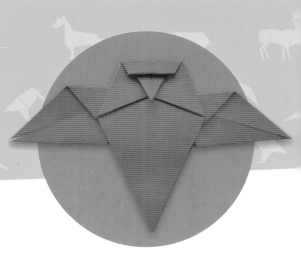

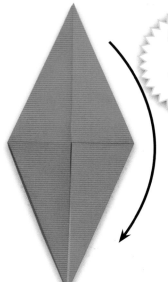

START WITH A BIRD BASE

Inner triangle

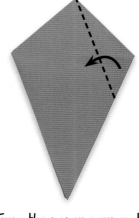

1 Find out how to make a bird base on pages 7-8. With the two open flaps pointing down, fold the upper top flap down to meet the bottom tip.

2 The inner triangle should now be revealed, as shown above.

3 Turn the paper over and repeat step 2 so that the inner triangle sticks up. Valley fold the right corner to the middle crease.

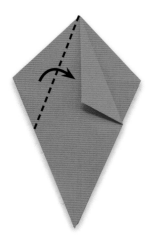

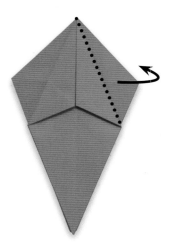

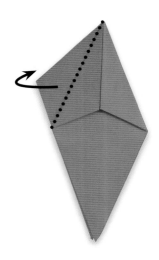

4 Do the same on the other side.

5 Mountain fold the right corner so that it folds back.

6 Do the same on the other side.

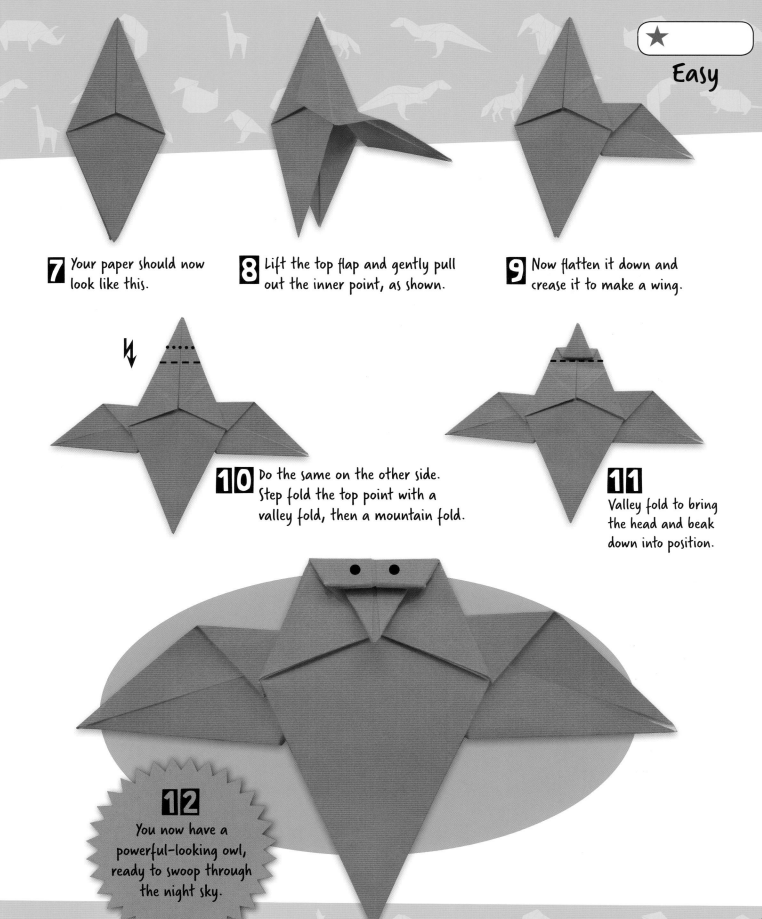

7 Your paper should now look like this.

8 Lift the top flap and gently pull out the inner point, as shown.

9 Now flatten it down and crease it to make a wing.

10 Do the same on the other side. Step fold the top point with a valley fold, then a mountain fold.

11 Valley fold to bring the head and beak down into position.

12 You now have a powerful-looking owl, ready to swoop through the night sky.

Dinosaurs

The dinosaurs lived millions of years ago. They weren't all big and fierce — they came in lots of different shapes and sizes. Check out these origami ones, from the terrible T. rex to the giant Diplodocus!

Baby Maiasaura

Diplodocus

Spiky plates!

Stegosaurus

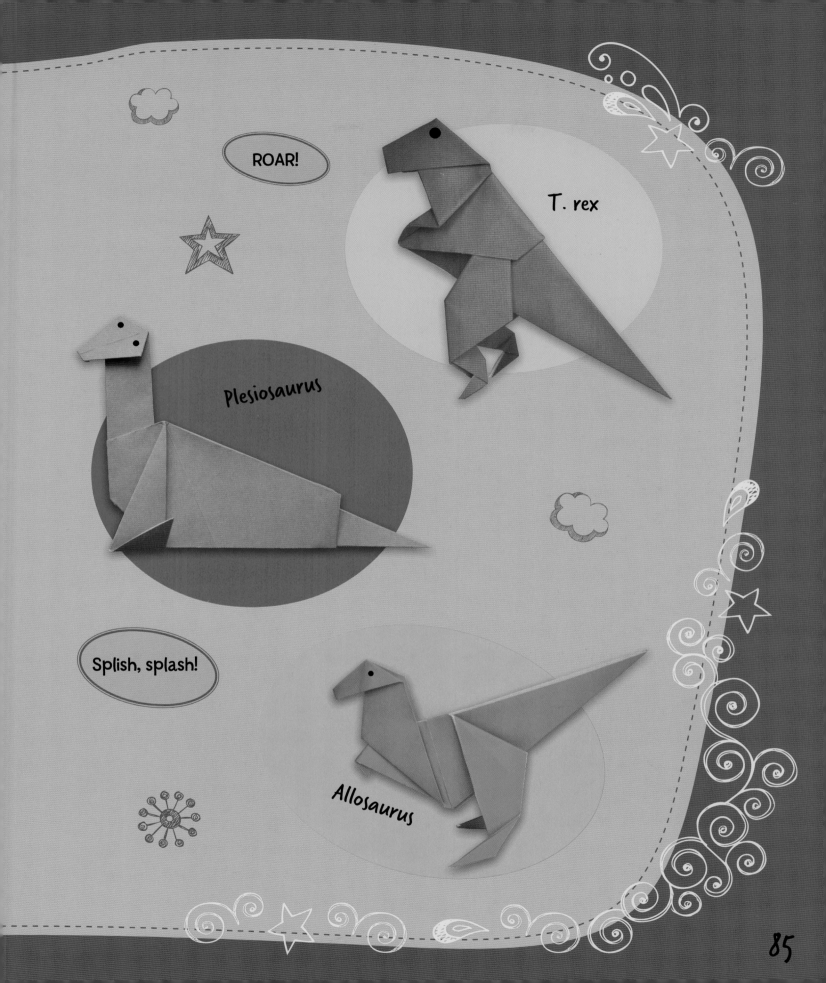

Baby Maiasaura

Maiasaura means "good mother lizard" because this dinosaur cared for its young and protected them from danger. Here's how to make one of Maiasaura's babies!

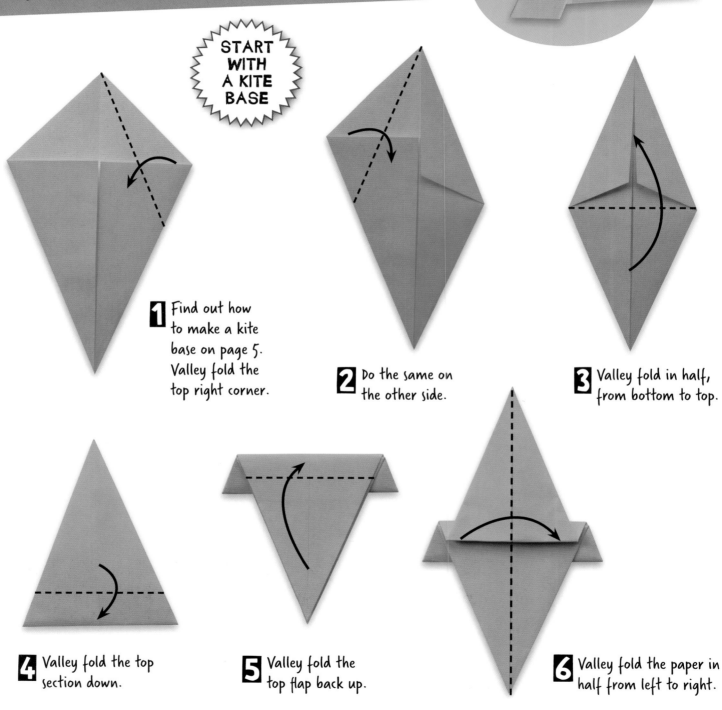

START WITH A KITE BASE

1 Find out how to make a kite base on page 5. Valley fold the top right corner.

2 Do the same on the other side.

3 Valley fold in half, from bottom to top.

4 Valley fold the top section down.

5 Valley fold the top flap back up.

6 Valley fold the paper in half from left to right.

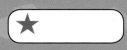
7 Turn the paper around to the position shown here. Mountain fold the left point.

8 Unfold, then make an inside reverse fold to create the head.

9 Tuck the tip of the nose in to make it blunt.

10 Your origami baby is finished. Why not try using a bigger piece of paper to make its parent?

Diplodocus

The Diplodocus was a huge plant-eating dinosaur. It may have used its long, powerful tail like a whip to strike at its enemies.

START WITH A KITE BASE

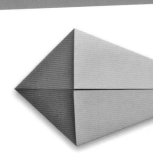

1 Find out how to make a kite base on page 5, starting with the white side facing down. Turn it on its side, as shown.

2 Turn the paper over. Valley fold the top section to the middle.

3 Do the same on the other side.

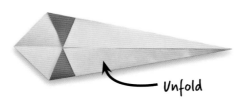

Unfold

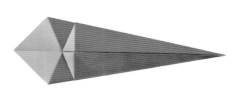

4 Unfold the upper flap on both sides.

5 Refold both flaps into valley folds.

6 The paper should now look like this.

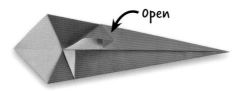

Open

7 Gently lift the corner of the top flap and open it out.

8 Now flatten the paper to form a triangle as shown.

9 Do the same on the other side.

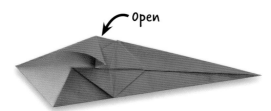

Open

10 Gently open out the left corner.

11 Flatten the paper into a triangle as shown, so that it slightly overlaps the triangle you made in step 8.

12 Do the same on the other side. Mountain fold in half, so that the bottom folds behind the top.

13 The flaps should point to the right. Fold the two flaps back to form the legs. Do the same on both sides.

14 Valley fold the right point so that it goes straight up.

15 Unfold, then make an inside reverse fold to create the neck.

16 Flatten the paper.

17 Mountain fold the right point.

18 Unfold, then make an inside reverse fold to create the head.

20 Stand up your cute origami Diplodocus — but watch out for that whipping tail!

19 Flatten the head and angle it a little bit. Tuck in the tip of the nose to make it blunt.

Allosaurus

Allosaurus was rather like its more famous cousin, T. rex. Although it wasn't quite as big in length or height, it was still a fearsome fighter!

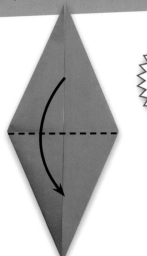

START WITH A BIRD BASE

1 Find out how to make a bird base on pages 7-8, and then place your paper like this. Valley fold the front flap.

2 Valley fold the paper in half from right to left. Turn it around so that the open flaps are on the right.

Peel back

3 Peel back the left flap to reveal the triangle underneath, as shown in step 4.

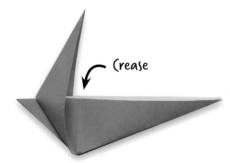

Crease

4 The edge of the upright piece should meet the crease on the body. Flatten the paper.

5 Valley fold the top point.

6 Unfold, then make an outside reverse fold to create the head.

7 Tuck the tip of the nose inside to make it blunt.

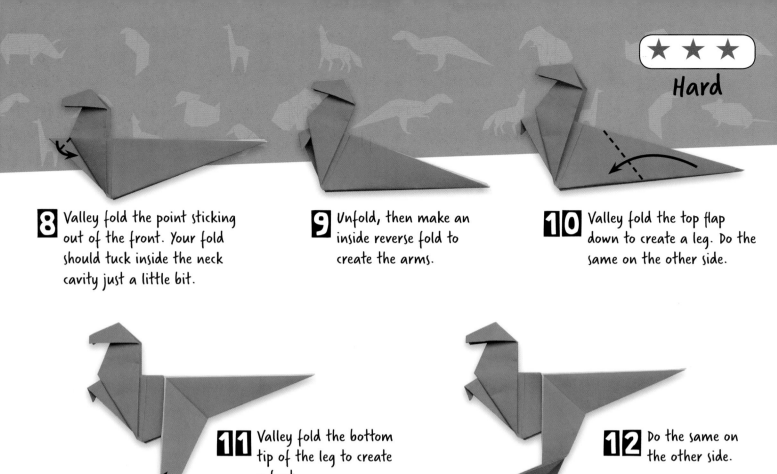

8 Valley fold the point sticking out of the front. Your fold should tuck inside the neck cavity just a little bit.

9 Unfold, then make an inside reverse fold to create the arms.

10 Valley fold the top flap down to create a leg. Do the same on the other side.

11 Valley fold the bottom tip of the leg to create a foot.

12 Do the same on the other side.

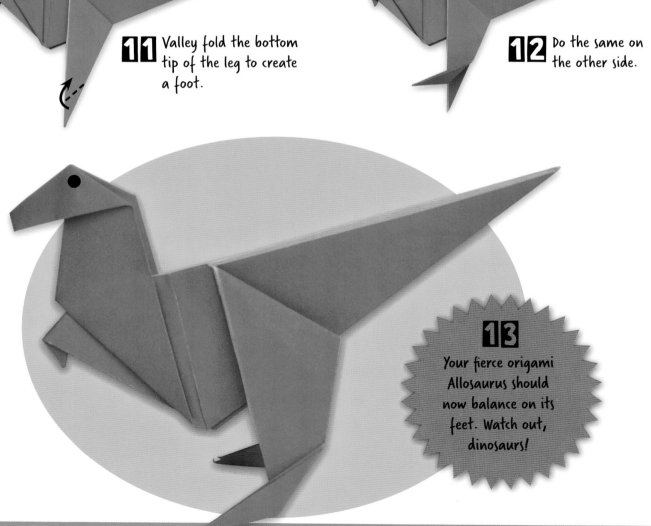

13 Your fierce origami Allosaurus should now balance on its feet. Watch out, dinosaurs!

Plesiosaurus

When dinosaurs were roaming the Earth, giant long-necked reptiles called plesiosaurs swam in the oceans. This one is called Plesiosaurus.

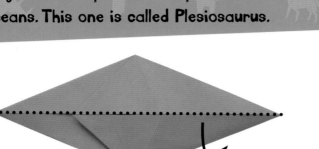

START WITH A FISH BASE

1 Find out how to make a fish base on page 6. With the flaps pointing to the left, mountain fold in half.

2 Valley fold the top flap in to the middle. Then do the same on the other side.

3 Valley fold the left point up.

4 Unfold, then make an inside reverse fold to create the neck. Make the neck stand straight up.

5 Mountain fold the upper flap of the neck inside itself, so that it becomes a narrow strip.

6 Do the same on the other side, this time using a valley fold.

7 Mountain fold the top point.

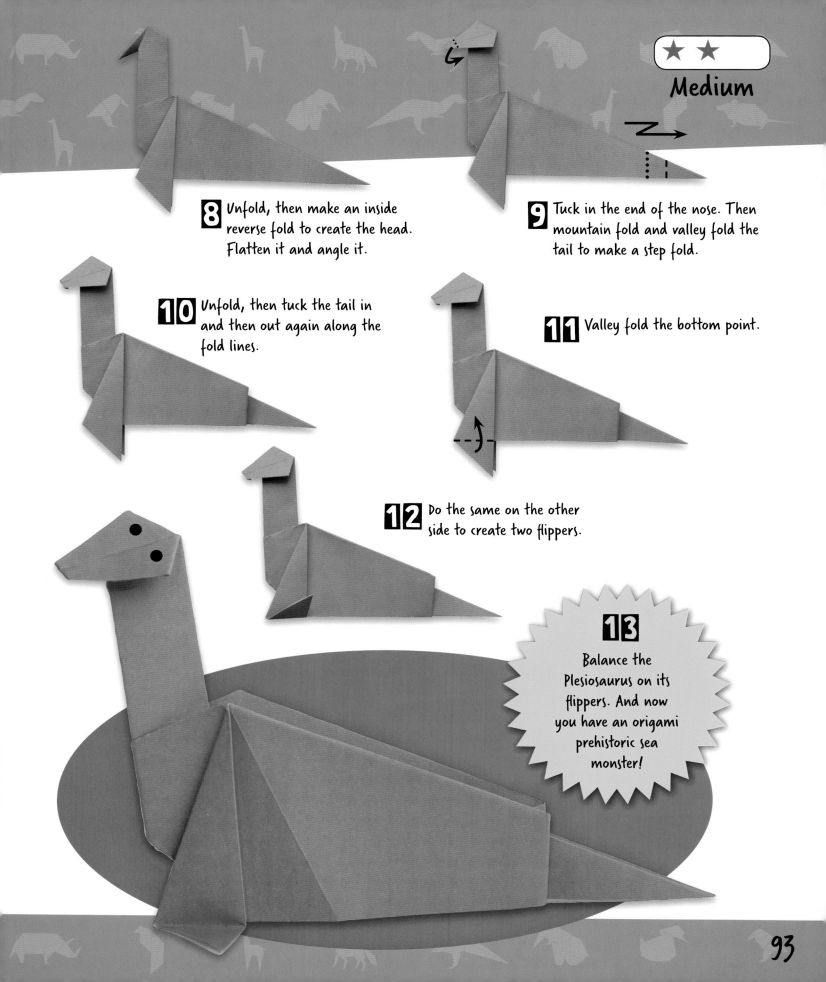

8 Unfold, then make an inside reverse fold to create the head. Flatten it and angle it.

9 Tuck in the end of the nose. Then mountain fold and valley fold the tail to make a step fold.

10 Unfold, then tuck the tail in and then out again along the fold lines.

11 Valley fold the bottom point.

12 Do the same on the other side to create two flippers.

13 Balance the Plesiosaurus on its flippers. And now you have an origami prehistoric sea monster!

Stegosaurus

Stegosaurus had two rows of spiky plates running along its back. They were used to help it keep warm – it turned them to the sun to warm up.

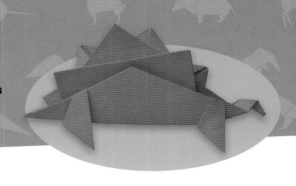

MAKE THE HEAD AND BODY

1 Turn your paper white side up. Valley fold in half and unfold.

2 Valley fold the right section to the middle crease.

3 Do the same on the other side.

4 Valley fold the top right corner.

5 Do the same on the other side.

6 Repeat steps 4 and 5 for the bottom corners.

7 Unfold all the corners so that the paper looks like this.

8 Open out the top right corner and make an inside reverse fold.

9 Do the same for the other corners. Valley fold the top right flap to overlap the left section slightly.

10 Valley fold the top left flap to overlap the right flap.

11 Repeat steps 9 and 10 for the bottom flaps.

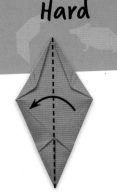

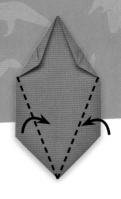

12 The paper should now look like this. Turn the paper over.

13 Valley fold the top edges.

14 Valley fold the right and left corners to meet in the middle.

15 Valley fold the paper in half from right to left.

16 Turn the paper as shown, so the feet are pointing down. Mountain fold the left point.

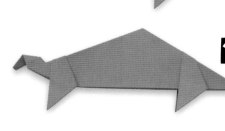

17 Unfold, then make an inside reverse fold to create the neck.

18 Mountain fold the left point.

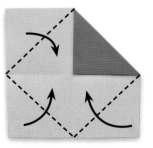

19 Now make an outside reverse fold to create the head. Tuck in the tip of the nose to make it blunt.

MAKE THE BACK

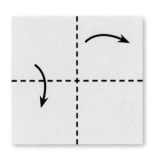

1 Start with your paper white side up. Valley fold into quarters.

2 Unfold, then valley fold the top right corner into the middle.

3 Do the same for the other three corners.

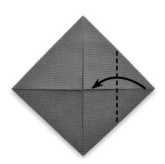

4 Valley fold the right corner into the middle.

Stegosaurus... continued

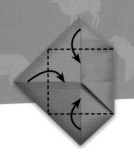

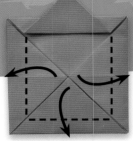

5 Do the same for the other corners.

6 Valley fold the top flap up.

7 Do the same for the other flaps.

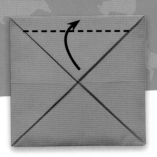

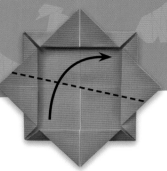

8 Valley fold the bottom section of the paper up at an angle, as shown, so that the triangles form an arc.

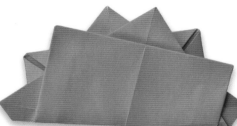

9 The paper should now look like this. This is the spiky back of the Stegosaurus.

PUT THE STEGOSAURUS TOGETHER

1 Slot the Stegosaurus's back into the body.

2 Stand the Stegosaurus up on its feet and you have one spiky origami dinosaur!

T. rex

Hard

Tyrannosaurus rex, or T. rex for short, was a fierce meat-eater with a big head and sharp teeth. Its name means "tyrant lizard king!"

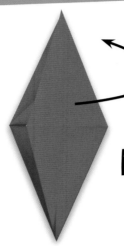

START WITH A BIRD BASE

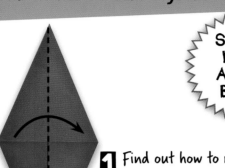

1 Find out how to make a bird base on pages 7-8, and then place your paper like this. Valley fold the upper flap.

2 Take the right flap at the very back of the paper and swing it to the left, so that two points are revealed at the top, as shown in step 3.

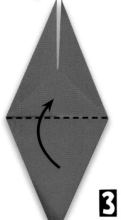

3 Valley fold the bottom flap up to the top.

4 Valley fold the bottom corner of the upper right flap into the middle.

5 Do the same on the other side.

6 The paper should now look like this. Turn the paper over.

Pull

7 Gently pull out the tall point on the right into the position shown in step 8.

T. rex... continued

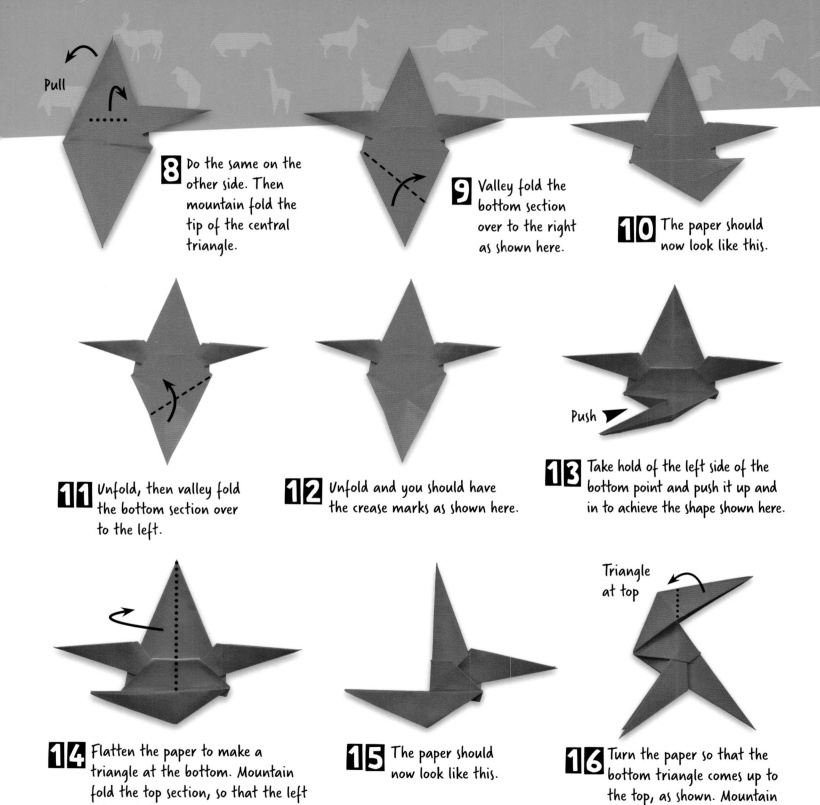

Pull

8 Do the same on the other side. Then mountain fold the tip of the central triangle.

9 Valley fold the bottom section over to the right as shown here.

10 The paper should now look like this.

11 Unfold, then valley fold the bottom section over to the left.

12 Unfold and you should have the crease marks as shown here.

Push

13 Take hold of the left side of the bottom point and push it up and in to achieve the shape shown here.

14 Flatten the paper to make a triangle at the bottom. Mountain fold the top section, so that the left side folds behind the right.

15 The paper should now look like this.

Triangle at top

16 Turn the paper so that the bottom triangle comes up to the top, as shown. Mountain fold the top point.

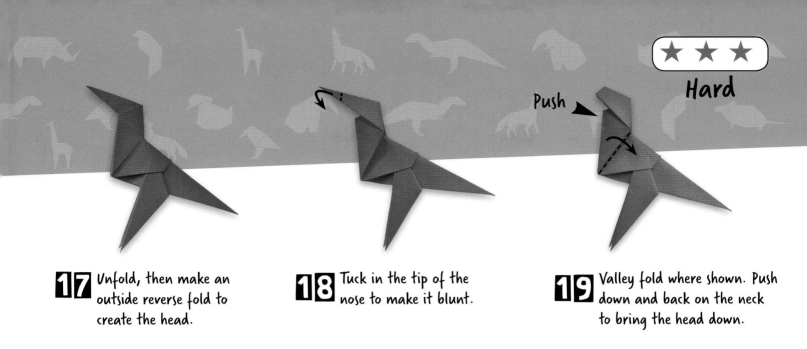

Push ►

17 Unfold, then make an outside reverse fold to create the head.

18 Tuck in the tip of the nose to make it blunt.

19 Valley fold where shown. Push down and back on the neck to bring the head down.

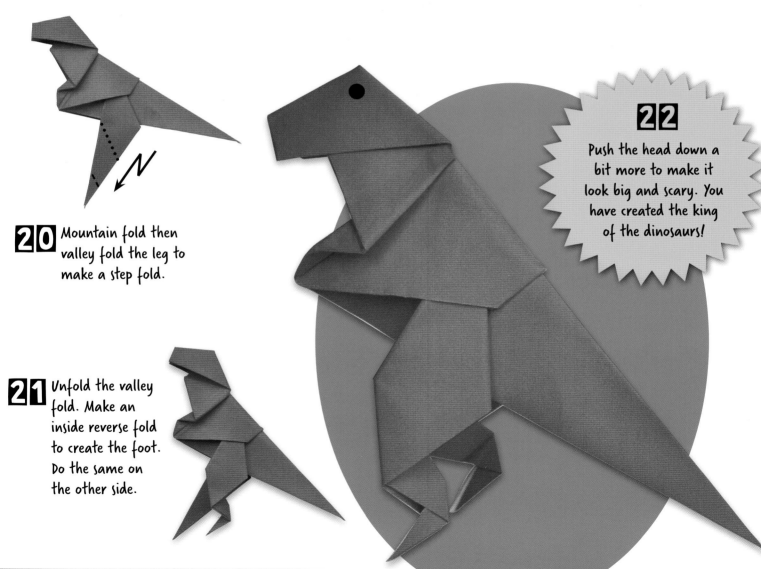

20 Mountain fold then valley fold the leg to make a step fold.

21 Unfold the valley fold. Make an inside reverse fold to create the foot. Do the same on the other side.

22 Push the head down a bit more to make it look big and scary. You have created the king of the dinosaurs!

ORIGAMI GIFTS

Gifts & boxes

Spoil someone special with a hand-made bookmark, photo frame, or a tulip. You could use the treat holder, envelope, or gift box to store a gift, giving it a personal touch.

Bookmark

Tulip

Gift bow

Cute!

Envelope

Surprise!

Photo frame

Gift box

Pretty basket

Pen holder

So sweet!

Treat holder

Star box

Cool!

Treat holder

This little pouch is perfect for holding treats! You could decorate the treat holder with hearts for Valentine's Day or balloons for a birthday gift.

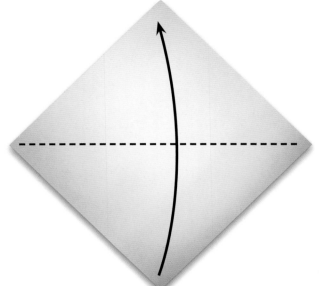

1 Start with your paper white side up. Valley fold your paper in half from bottom to top.

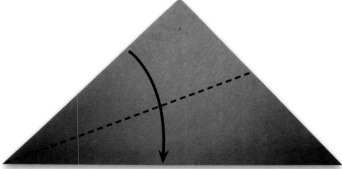

2 Valley fold the top triangle down so that the left side meets the bottom. Crease well and then unfold.

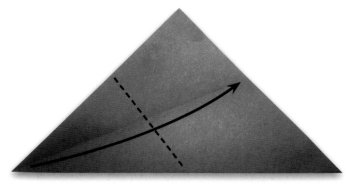

3 Valley fold the bottom-left point over to the right so that it meets the far end of the previous fold.

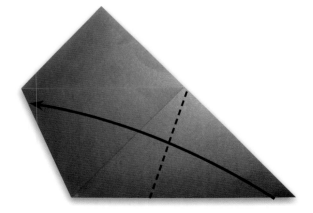

4 Valley fold the bottom-right point over to the left to meet the left point.

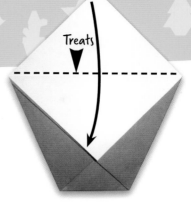

5 Valley fold the top flap of the triangle down to create your pocket.

6 Your model should look like this. Decorate the model if you like then place your treats inside the pocket. Fold the top triangle down to close it.

Treats

7

Use a special sticker or stamp to seal your treat box before you give it away.

Bookmark

If you know someone who loves to read, you could make them this pretty origami bookmark. What a fun way to mark the pages of a book you love!

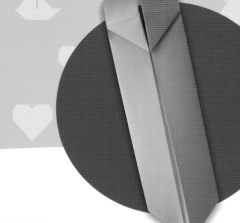

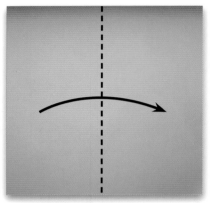

1 Place the paper as shown and valley fold in half from left to right. Crease and then unfold.

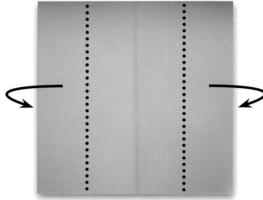

2 Mountain fold the left and right sides in half to create a rectangle.

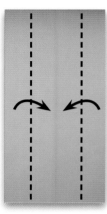

3 Valley fold the left and right sides in half. Crease well and then unfold.

4 Valley fold the top left corner to meet the first left fold, crease, and then unfold.

5 Using the bottom point of the corner fold of step 4 as a guide, mountain fold the top of the paper behind your rectangle and crease well.

6 Valley fold the top left and right corners into the middle.

7 Mountain fold the top triangle to create a straight top.

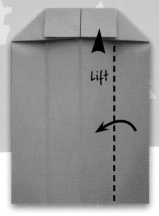

Lift

Lift

Close-up of top folds.

8 Valley fold the right side in half and at the same time lift the top right section up. Flatten the top section.

9 Your paper should now look like this. Repeat step 8 on the left side.

10 Valley fold each of the top four corners.

11 Valley fold the bottom two corners to shape the bottom of your bookmark.

12 Your model should look like this. Turn your model over.

13 Your bookmark is ready! Why not pair it with a book as a gift?

Envelope

This elegant envelope will look amazing with a personalized greeting card or a handwritten letter inside it.

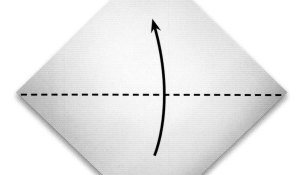

1 Place the paper as shown and valley fold in half from bottom to top.

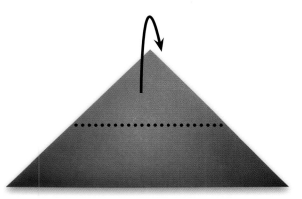

2 Mountain fold the top flap in half horizontally and tuck it behind itself.

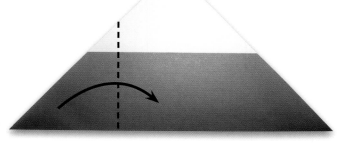

3 Valley fold the left point over to the right.

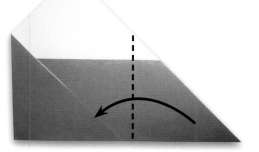

4 Valley fold the right point over to the left side. Make sure this fold is the same size as the fold from step 3.

5 Valley fold the top flap over to the right where it crosses the bottom flap.

6 Lift up the triangle you have just created so that it points toward you.

Lift

Press

7 Press the triangle point down to flatten it into a square.

8 Valley fold the top point down and tuck it into the little square flap to close the envelope.

9
Carefully open the envelope and place a card or letter inside it, closing it when you've finished.

Merry Christmas!

Tulip

This tulip may be tricky to make, but it is really pretty and makes a lovely gift for someone special.

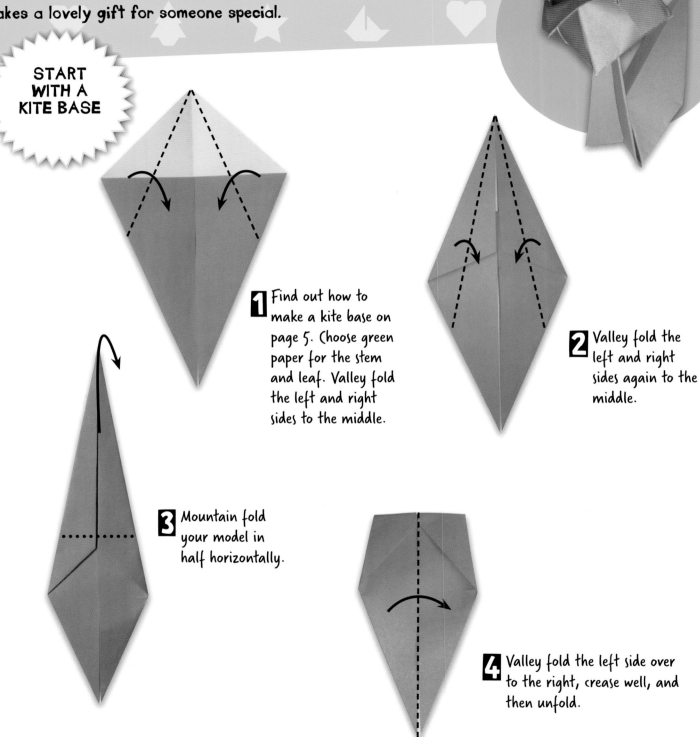

START WITH A KITE BASE

1 Find out how to make a kite base on page 5. Choose green paper for the stem and leaf. Valley fold the left and right sides to the middle.

2 Valley fold the left and right sides again to the middle.

3 Mountain fold your model in half horizontally.

4 Valley fold the left side over to the right, crease well, and then unfold.

5 Unfold the mountain fold from step 3. Turn your model over so it looks like the picture in step 6.

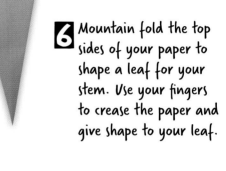

6 Mountain fold the top sides of your paper to shape a leaf for your stem. Use your fingers to crease the paper and give shape to your leaf.

7 Valley fold the bottom point up to complete your stem.

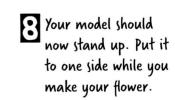

8 Your model should now stand up. Put it to one side while you make your flower.

Tulip... continued

START
WITH A
WATERBOMB
BASE

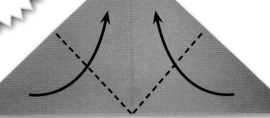

9 Find out how to make a waterbomb base on page 7. Choose pink or yellow paper for the petals. Place your waterbomb base with the point at the top. Valley fold the top left and right points up into the middle.

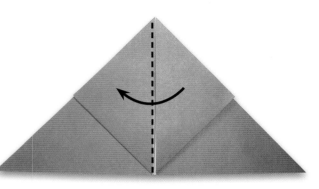

10 Valley fold the top right flap over to the left.

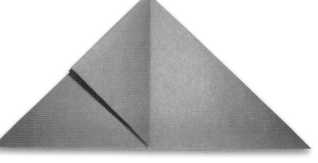

11 Your paper should now look like this. Turn it over and repeat steps 9 and 10 on the reverse.

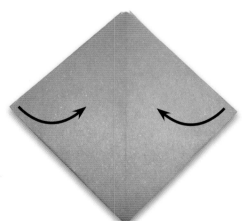

Close-up of flaps.

12 Take the top left and right flaps and slot the right flap into the pocket of the left flap as far as you can.

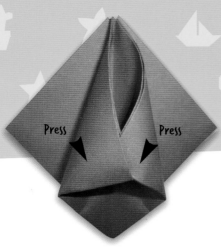

Press   Press

13 Your model should look like this. Carefully press down to flatten the paper, making sure the sides are equal.

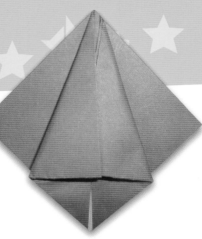

14 Your model should look like this. Turn it over and repeat steps 12 and 13 on the reverse.

Hold here

Blow here

15 Your model should look like this. Blow gently into the bottom end to inflate your tulip.

16 Your model should now look like this. Gently pull back the top layers to create petals.

17 Your model should now look like this.

18 To finish your tulip, carefully place your flower on the finished stem from step 8. Isn't it pretty?

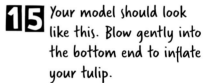

Gift box

Fill this pretty little gift box with treats to make a lovely present.

START WITH A BLINTZ BASE

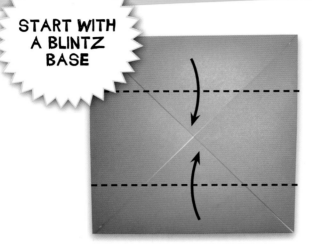

1 Find out how to make a blintz base on page 5. Valley fold the top and bottom sides into the middle, crease well, and then unfold.

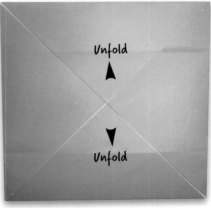

2 Unfold the top and bottom triangles.

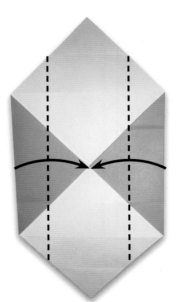

3 Valley fold the left and right sides into the middle.

4 Valley fold the top and bottom diagonally, crease well, and then unfold.

5 Valley fold the top and bottom diagonally again, but in the other direction, crease well, and then unfold.

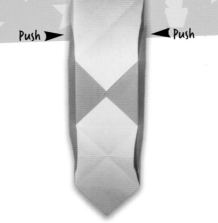

Open ◀ ━━▶ Open

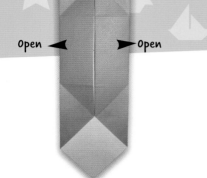

Push ▶ ◀ Push

Push ▶ ◀ Push

6 Now open the left and right flaps so that they are pointing upward.

7 Your model should look like this. Push in the top of the sides to collapse them.

8 Valley fold the top while pushing in the sides to form another side of your box.

9 Valley fold the top to complete the side and bottom. Use your fingers to flatten the top to the side and bottom.

10 Your model should now look like this. Repeat steps 7, 8, and 9 on the remaining side.

11 Your box should now look like this. To create a lid, use a slightly bigger piece of paper and repeat steps 1 to 10.

12 Fill your box with treats. Add the bow on page 114 to make it even more special.

Gift bow

Attach this striking bow to any gift to add a personal, stylish touch!

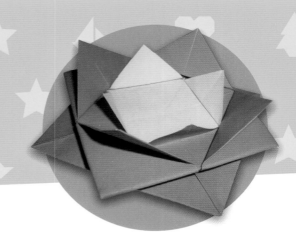

START WITH A BLINTZ BASE

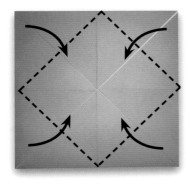

1 Find out how to make a blintz base on page 5. Place your base so that the flaps are facing up. Fold the points into the middle.

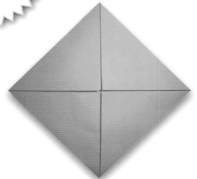

2 Your model should look like this. Turn your model over.

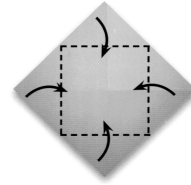

3 Fold the points into the middle, as you would to make a blintz base.

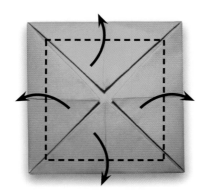

4 Valley fold the flaps out, so that they overlap the edges.

5 Your model should look like this. Turn your model over.

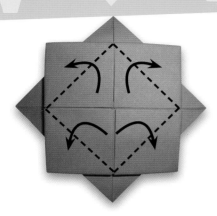

6 Valley fold and lift the top flaps so that they point upward.

7 Valley fold and lift the bottom flaps so that they point upward.

8 Your gift bow is ready. You can write a greeting inside for a personal touch.

Happy Birthday!

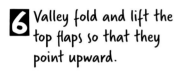

9 Why not use your bow to decorate your gift box from page 112?

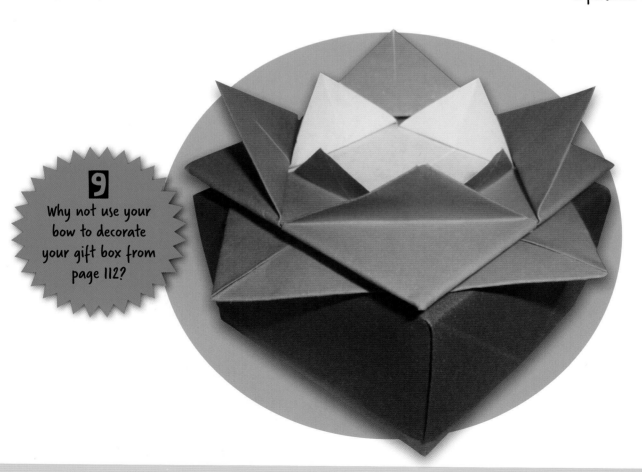

Photo frame

Put a picture of friends or your pet in this pretty photo frame. It will certainly brighten up any room.

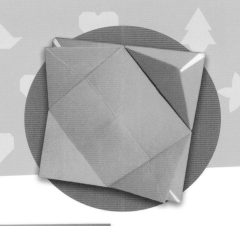

START WITH A BLINTZ BASE

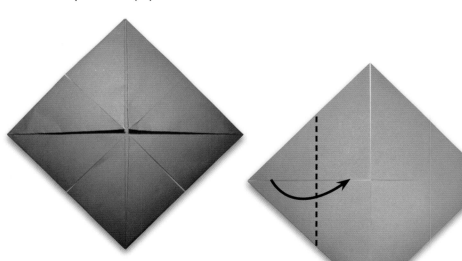

1 Find out how to make a blintz base on page 5. Place flap-side down. Valley fold the left point into the middle.

2 Do the same with the three remaining points.

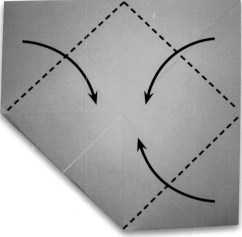

3 Turn your model so that one corner is pointing toward you. It should now look like this.

4 Turn your model over and valley fold the left point into the middle.

5 Repeat step 4 with the three remaining points.

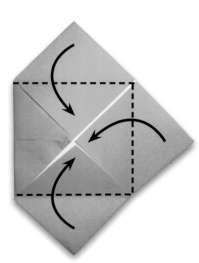

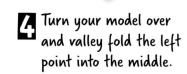

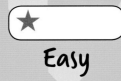

Easy

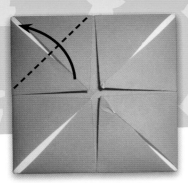

6 Turn over your model and valley fold the top left flap out to the top left corner.

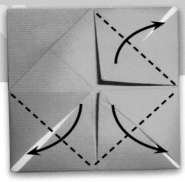

7 Do the same with the three remaining flaps.

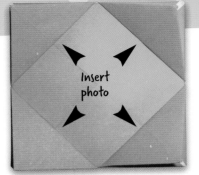

Insert photo

8 Insert your photo into the frame by slotting it into the corners.

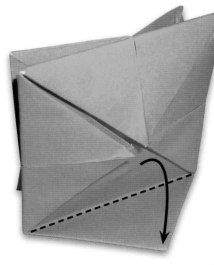

9 Use the bottom flap at the back of your frame to stand the frame up.

10 Your frame is now ready to display. You could make one for each member of your family!

Pen holder

Keep your pens neat and tidy in this handy origami pen holder. You'll never lose a pen again!

1 Place your paper as shown and valley fold in half, crease well, then unfold.

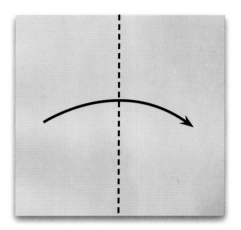

2 Valley fold the left side into the middle. Crease well and then unfold.

3 Do the same to the right side.

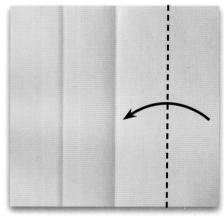

4 Valley fold the top corner into the middle of the paper.

5 Valley fold the top corner of the far right panel.

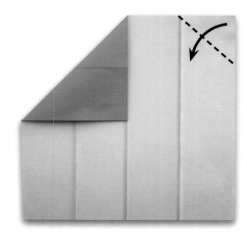

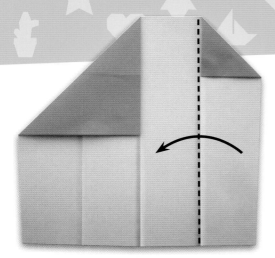

6 Valley fold the right panel into the middle of the paper.

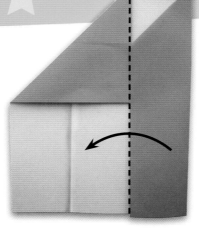

7 Valley fold the right panel again.

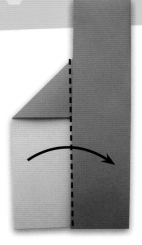

8 Valley fold the left panel over to the right.

Close-up of bottom fold.

9 Valley fold the bottom edge of the pen holder to close it.

10 Turn over your pen holder. Now you can keep your pens neat and tidy!

Pretty basket

This little basket will make a great storage container for all your hair ties and bobby pins.

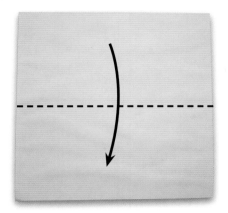

1 To make the handle, valley fold the paper in half, crease well, then unfold.

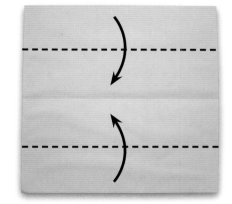

2 Valley fold the top and bottom sides into the middle.

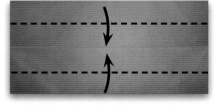

3 Valley fold the top and bottom sides again into the middle.

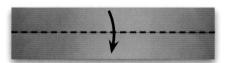

4 Valley fold the paper in half. Crease well.

5 Valley fold the paper in half again.

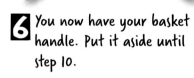

6 You now have your basket handle. Put it aside until step 10.

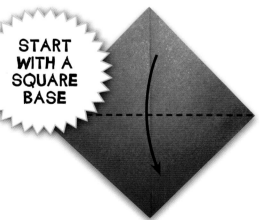

7 See how to make a square base on page 5. Turn so the open ends are at the top. Valley fold the top flap in half to the bottom.

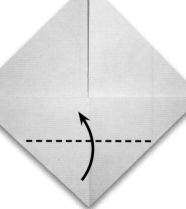

8 Valley fold the flap up again to the middle.

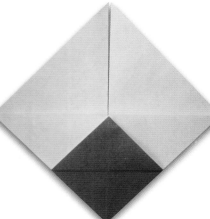

9 Turn the model over and repeat steps 7 and 8 on the other side.

Slide

10 Slide one side of the handle into the middle of the small triangles as far as it will go.

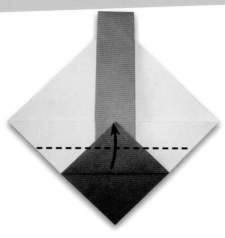

11 Holding the handle firmly in place, fold the small triangle flap and the handle up to the central fold.

12 Turn over the paper and repeat steps 10 and 11 on the other side.

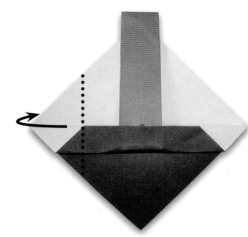

13 Mountain fold the upper left side in half so that the point touches the inside crease.

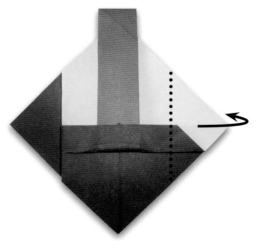

14 Do the same on the upper right side.

15 Turn over the paper and repeat steps 13 and 14 on this side.

Pretty basket... continued

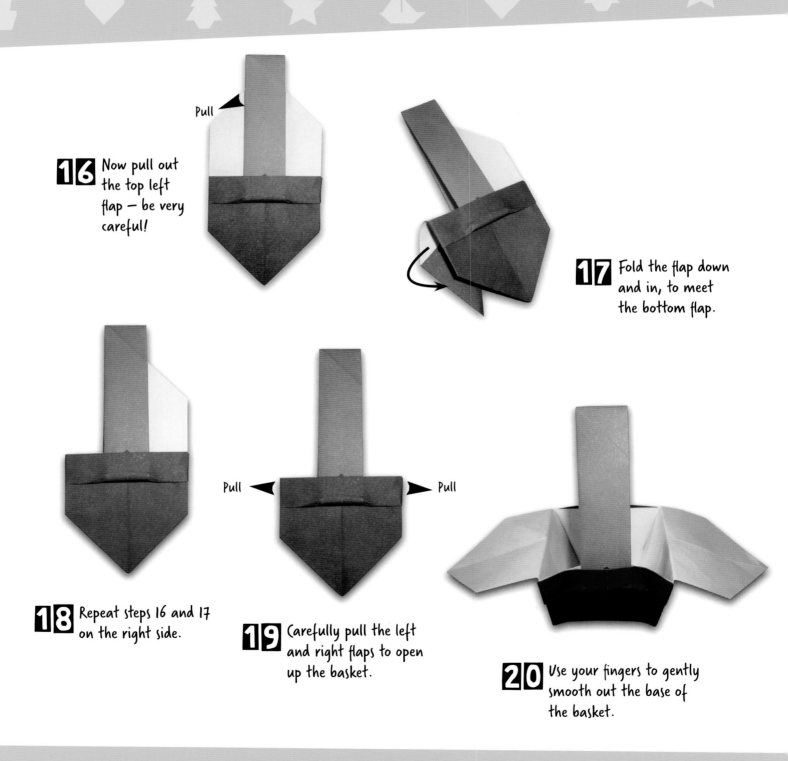

Pull

16 Now pull out the top left flap — be very careful!

17 Fold the flap down and in, to meet the bottom flap.

18 Repeat steps 16 and 17 on the right side.

Pull   Pull

19 Carefully pull the left and right flaps to open up the basket.

20 Use your fingers to gently smooth out the base of the basket.

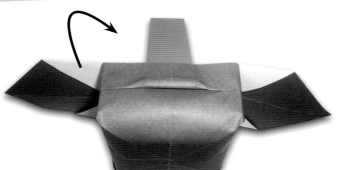

21 The model should now look like this. Fold the left flap into the basket base.

22 Smooth the left flap down and then fold the right flap in and smooth down.

23 Fill your pretty basket with things like hair ties, pins, and clips.

Star box

This pretty box draws attention to its contents.
You could use it to store beads, paper clips, or buttons.

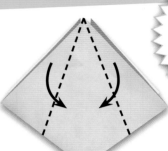

START WITH A SQUARE BASE

1 See how to make a square base on page 6. Make it so that the orange is on the inside. Turn the base so that the open part is at the top. Valley fold the two top flaps to meet the central crease.

2 Your model should now look like this. Turn it over and repeat step 1.

3 Valley fold each flap and crease it well.

4 Gently tease out the top right flap, as shown. Flatten the flap. Repeat on the left flap.

5 Your model should now look like this. Turn over the paper.

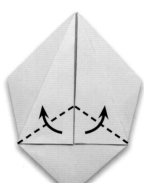

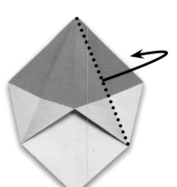

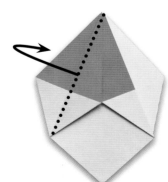

6 Valley fold the top flaps.

7 Your model should look like this. Repeat step 4.

8 Take the top-right flap and mountain fold it behind itself.

9 Do the same on the left side.

10 Your model now looks like this. Turn it over and repeat steps 8 and 9.

11 Valley fold the bottom, and crease well along the fold. Unfold.

12 Valley fold down the top flap.

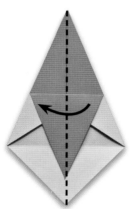

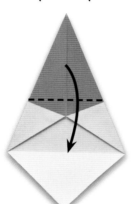

13 Valley fold the top right flap over to the left. Then repeat step 12.

14 Turn over the paper and repeat steps 12 and 13.

15 Your model should now look like this.

16 Turn the model so that it looks like this from above. Pull out the four pointed flaps.

17 Gently push the bottom of the box from the inside into shape. Your star box is ready — what will you keep in it?

Toys

From puppets and boats to pretty fans and ninja stars, in this chapter you can have lots of fun making and playing with amazing origami toys!

Pretty fan

Fox puppet

Ooh la la!

Swooping Butterfly

Super spinner

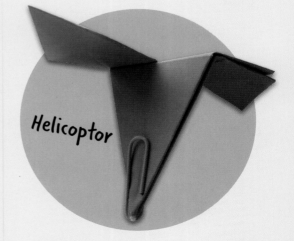

Helicoptor

Ninja star

Fortune teller

Whoosh!

Funky boats

Cute!

Hang glider

Windmill

127

Pretty fan

This stylish fan will keep you cool on a warm summer's day. You won't ever feel hot and sticky again!

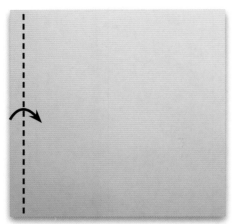

1 Place your paper white side up. Valley fold the paper toward the middle, starting at the left side.

2 Mountain fold the left side and crease well.

3 Continue to step fold (mountain and valley fold next to each other) until you have no paper left.

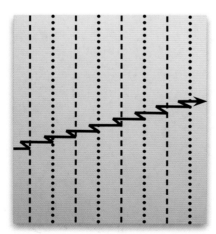

4 Valley fold the bottom end to create the handle of the fan.

Pull ▶

◀ Pull

5 Gently pull the edges of your model to expand your fan.

Ribbon ▶

6 Tie a ribbon around the bottom of your fan for decoration.

7
Wave your fan to feel a breeze. Why not try different-sized fans? Use larger paper for a more effective fan.

Ninja star

This ninja star will make a cool pattern as it flies through the air, but don't throw it at people!

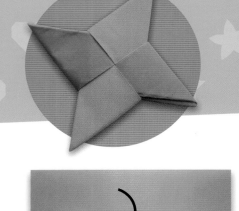

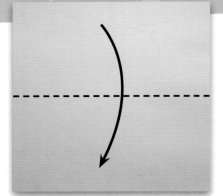

1 Place your paper as shown. Valley fold in half, crease well, then unfold.

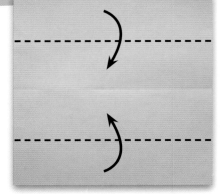

2 Valley fold the top and bottom sides in half, creasing the paper well.

3 Valley fold your paper in half again.

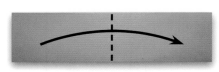

4 Valley fold the paper in half, crease well, then unfold it.

5 Repeat steps 1 to 6 with another piece of paper. This can be the same shade or a different one.

6 Valley fold the left and right corners of your pieces of paper diagonally and crease well.

7 Valley fold the left side of the yellow paper down toward the middle fold. Do the same with the blue paper, but fold it upward.

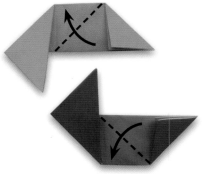

8 Repeat step 7 with the right sides of each piece of paper, but fold the blue paper down and the yellow paper up.

9 Your models should look like this.

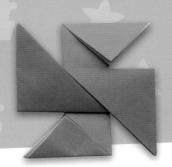

10 Turn the yellow model over and position the blue model in its middle.

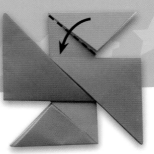

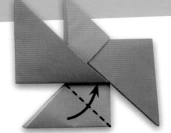

11 Valley fold the top yellow triangle down and tuck the point into the left blue triangle.

12 Valley fold the bottom yellow triangle up and tuck it into the right blue triangle.

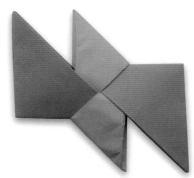

13 Your model should now look like this. Check that everything is tucked in and well creased.

14 Turn your model over, it should look like this. Valley fold the right blue triangle down and tuck it into the bottom yellow triangle.

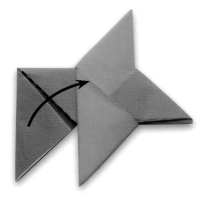

15 Valley fold the left blue triangle up and tuck it into the top yellow triangle.

16 Hold your ninja star with one hand and flick your wrist to throw it — how far did it go?

Funky boats

Even though you cannot put them in the water,
you will have lots of fun playing with these origami boats.

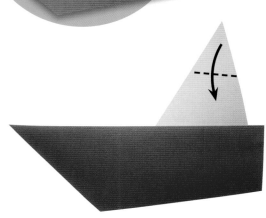

1 To make a tugboat, place your paper as shown and valley fold in half diagonally.

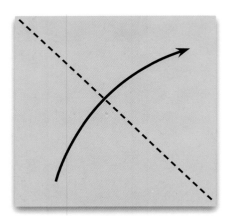

2 Valley fold the bottom point up at an angle, then turn this fold into an inside reverse fold. See page 4 if you need help.

3 Your paper should look like this. Now valley fold down the top point.

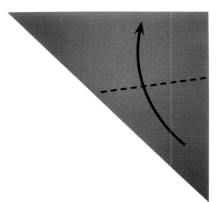

4 Turn this fold into an inside reverse fold to create your boat's cabin.

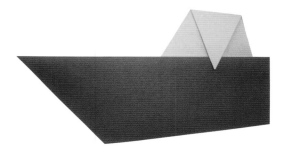

5 Add windows to your cabin and decorate the hull to make it ready to set sail.

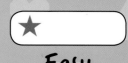

Easy

1 To make a sailboat, valley fold your paper in half diagonally.

2 Valley fold the left point up to the top point, crease well, and unfold.

3 Valley fold the right point up to the top point, crease well, and unfold.

4 Valley fold the front flap down to the bottom.

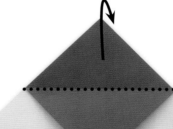

5 Mountain fold the back flap down to the bottom of the reverse side.

8 Turn your sailboat around. It is ready to cast off!

6 Valley fold the left and right points up again so they meet in the middle.

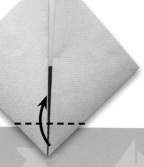

7 Valley fold the bottom point up to create a stand for your boat.

Super spinner

When this super spinner rolls around, the different sections will make a fantastic pattern!

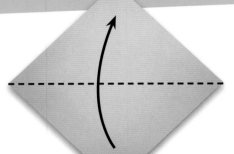

1 Start with your paper white side up and valley fold it in half diagonally.

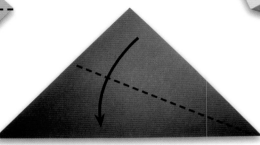

2 Valley fold the top point down so that the right side meets the bottom side, crease, and unfold.

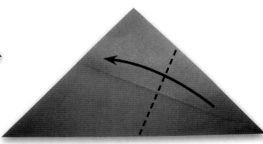

3 Valley fold the right point to the left side using the previous fold as your guide. Crease well.

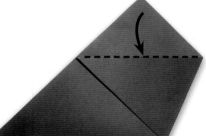

4 Valley fold the top flap into the pocket created by the last fold.

Close-up of pocket fold.

5 Your first section is now ready. Repeat steps 1 to 5 with six more pieces of paper in different shades.

6 When all seven sections are complete, you are ready to assemble your spinner.

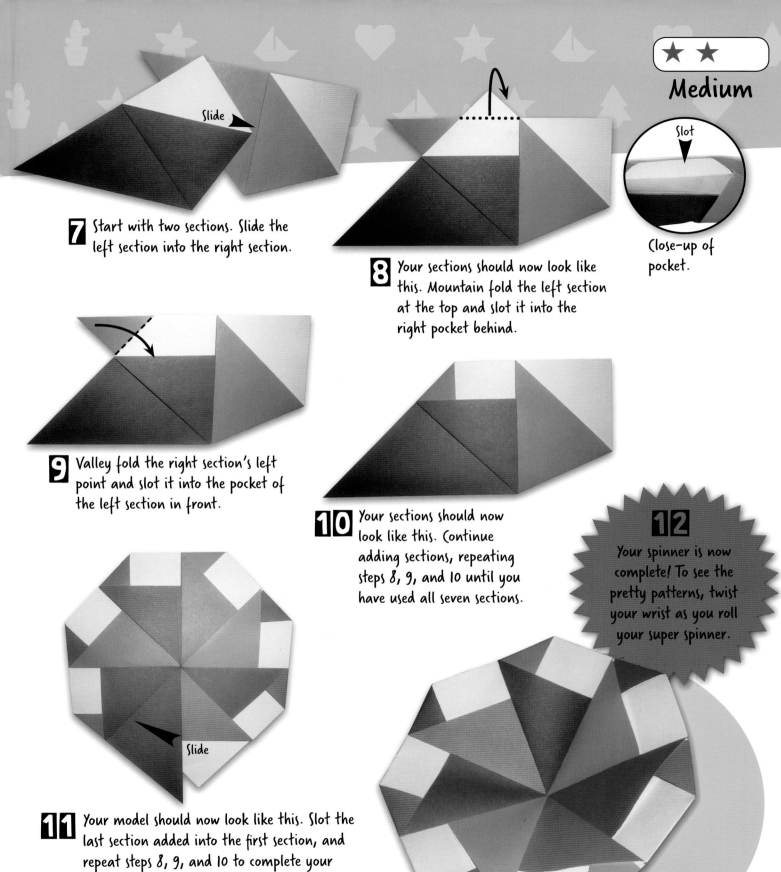

Slide

7 Start with two sections. Slide the left section into the right section.

Slot

Close-up of pocket.

8 Your sections should now look like this. Mountain fold the left section at the top and slot it into the right pocket behind.

9 Valley fold the right section's left point and slot it into the pocket of the left section in front.

10 Your sections should now look like this. Continue adding sections, repeating steps 8, 9, and 10 until you have used all seven sections.

12 Your spinner is now complete! To see the pretty patterns, twist your wrist as you roll your super spinner.

Slide

11 Your model should now look like this. Slot the last section added into the first section, and repeat steps 8, 9, and 10 to complete your spinner. You will need to create a slight cone shape to do this.

Swooping Butterfly

A butterfly has four wings, and the patterns on the right side are symmetrical with the patterns on the left. You could decorate yours after you make it!

1 Start with the paper white side up. Valley fold it in half and open it up. Then valley fold it in half the other way and open it again.

2 Valley fold the paper diagonally and open it up. Fold it diagonally the other way and open it again.

3 Valley fold the top right corner. Fold the other corners in the same way.

4 Valley fold the top right corner again.

5 Fold the other corners in the same way.

6 You should now have a small square, like this.

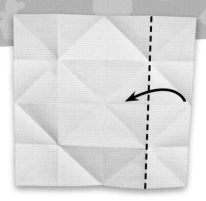

7 Unfold your paper completely. Valley fold the right section.

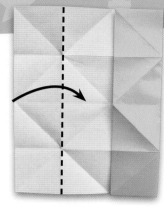

8 Valley fold the left section to meet in the middle.

9 Your paper should now look like this.

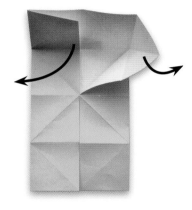

10 Take the top corners and gently pull them open, so that the top folds down.

11 Keep pulling the corners out and bringing the top down, so that this shape appears.

12 Flatten the paper as shown. Then turn it so that the top becomes the bottom.

13 Repeat steps 10 and 11 to get the shape in this picture. Mountain fold the top section back.

14 Valley fold the upper right flap.

15 Do the same on the other side.

Butterfly... continued

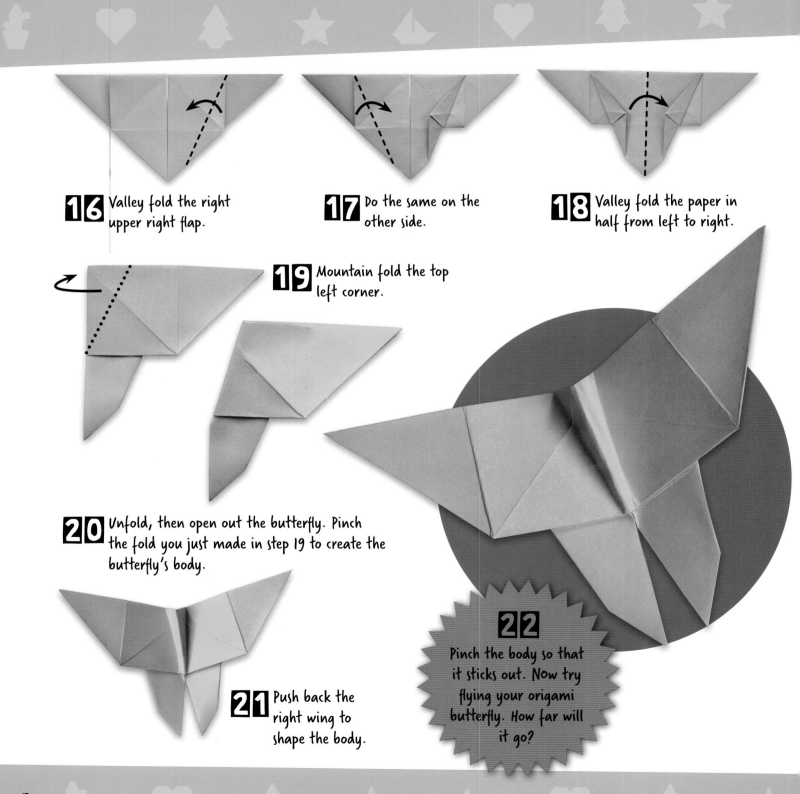

16 Valley fold the right upper right flap.

17 Do the same on the other side.

18 Valley fold the paper in half from left to right.

19 Mountain fold the top left corner.

20 Unfold, then open out the butterfly. Pinch the fold you just made in step 19 to create the butterfly's body.

21 Push back the right wing to shape the body.

22 Pinch the body so that it sticks out. Now try flying your origami butterfly. How far will it go?

Fortune teller

Medium

How many gifts will you get? When will you go on a trip?
Find out the answers by using your fortune teller!

START WITH A BLINTZ BASE

1 Find out how to make a blintz base on page 5. Turn it over so that the flaps are facing down.

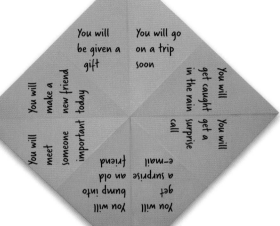

2 Write your eight fortunes in the eight individual sections.

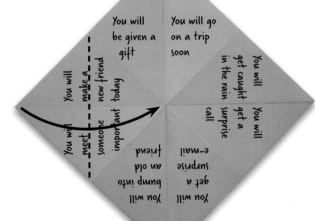

3 Valley fold the left point into the middle.

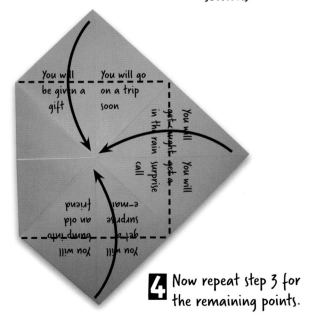

4 Now repeat step 3 for the remaining points.

Fortune teller... continued

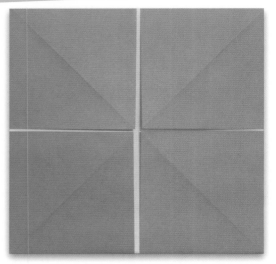

5 Your paper should now look like this. Write the numbers 1 to 8 on the different sections.

6 Turn your paper over and draw a square onto each corner of your fortune teller in a different shade.

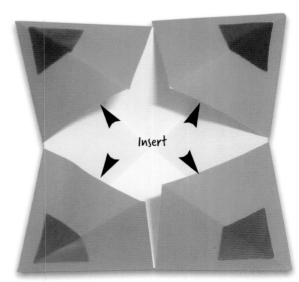

7 Use your fingers to carefully lift up the flaps in the middle.

8 Insert your thumb and forefingers into the pockets you have created.

9 Your model should now look like this.

How to use your fortune teller

1. Insert your fingers into the fortune teller.
2. Ask your friend to choose a shade.
3. Spell out the chosen shade and, as you do this, open and close the fortune teller.
4. When you've finished spelling you will be left with four numbers showing on the fortune teller. Ask your friend to choose between the four numbers.
5. Count out the number, opening and closing the fortune teller.
6. When you've finished counting, you will see four numbers. Ask your friend to choose one of them.
7. Open the fortune teller and read the fortune underneath that number.

10 Your fortune teller is now ready to use. Try it out on your friends.

Fox puppet

This fox has extra large ears so that he can hear everything!
Why not use this idea and write your own puppet show?

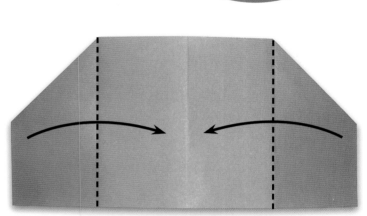

START WITH AN ORGAN BASE

1 Find out how to make an organ base on page 8. Your organ base should look like this. Now turn it over.

2 Valley fold the left and right sides into the middle.

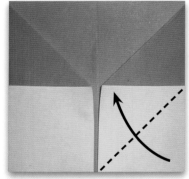

3 Valley fold the bottom right corner into the middle.

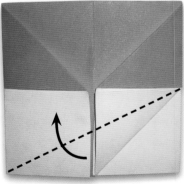

4 Valley fold the whole of the top flap diagonally.

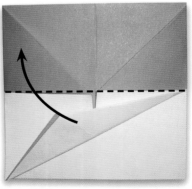

5 Valley fold the top flap again horizontally.

6 Your model should now look like this.

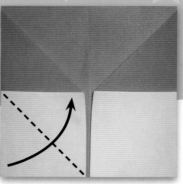

7 Turn over your model and valley fold the bottom-left corner into the middle.

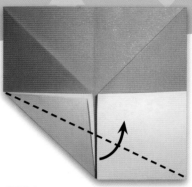

8 Valley fold the whole of the bottom flap diagonally.

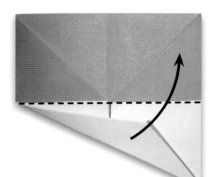

9 Valley fold again horizontally.

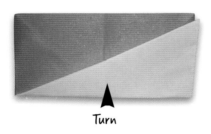

Turn

10 Your paper should look like this. Turn your model over.

open

11 Your model should look like this from above. Now open the pocket at the bottom with your fingers.

Push

12 Turn the paper over. Push the middle in gently with your finger to create the mouth.

Pull   Pull

13 Pull out the ears of the fox. Insert your fingers in the pockets behind to make the nose and mouth stick out.

14

Draw on the fox's features. You can move the fox's mouth by putting your fingers into the back and moving them carefully.

Hang glider

Although you can't use this hang glider to fly through the air, you will have great fun making and playing with it.

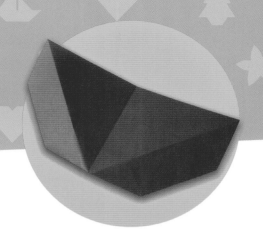

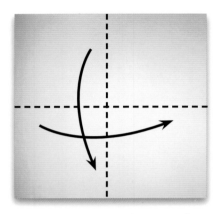

1 Place your paper as shown and valley fold in half from top to bottom. Crease and unfold. Valley fold your paper in half from left to right, crease, and then unfold.

2 Valley fold the top down to the middle fold made in step 1.

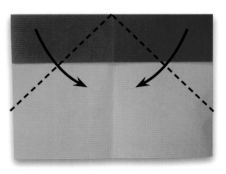

3 Valley fold the top left and right corners into the middle, crease well, and then unfold.

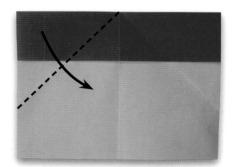

4 Take the top-left corner and make an inside reverse fold along the top edge, bringing the corner into the middle. See page 4 for help on how to do an inside reverse fold.

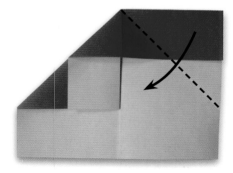

5 Your model should now look like this. Repeat step 4 on the top-right hand corner.

6 Valley fold the top point down and crease well.

Close-up of pockets.

7 Valley fold the two white triangle flaps up and slot them into the pockets of the central red triangle.

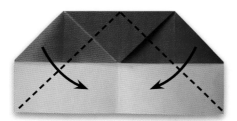

8 Valley fold the left and right sides to shape the wings. Crease well and then unfold.

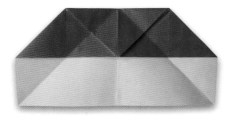

9 Your model should look like this. Turn it over and add a paper clip to the middle to weigh it down.

10 Your glider is now ready to fly! Throw it and watch it soar through the air!

Windmill

You can blow on this windmill to watch it spin or you can stand it in a plant and wait for a breeze to turn it.

1 Place your paper as shown. Valley fold in half from bottom to top and left to right. Crease and unfold.

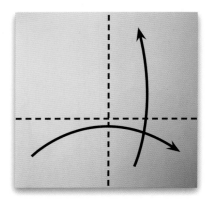

2 Valley fold your paper in half on both diagonals. Crease well and unfold.

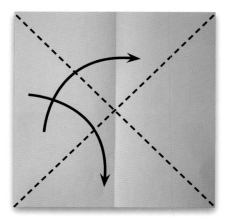

3 Valley fold the left and right sides so they meet in the middle.

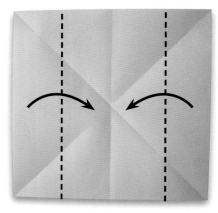

4 Valley fold the top and bottom edges up into the middle, crease well, and then unfold.

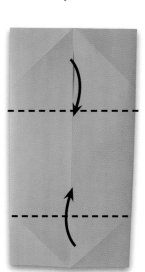

5 Valley fold the top left and right flaps out to the sides. This will pull the paper behind them upward.

6 Your model should look like this. Pull the top flap down so that it lies flat.

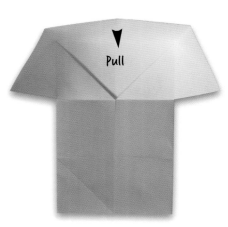

Pull

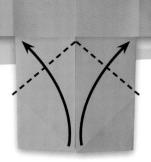

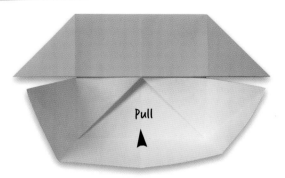

7 Valley fold the bottom-left and bottom-right flaps out to the sides.

Pull

8 Your model should look like this. Pull the bottom flap up so that it lies flat.

9 Valley fold the bottom-left triangle down.

11

Ask an adult to help you attach your windmill to a pencil so that you can hold it or stand it up. Blow gently on it to see it turn.

10 Valley fold the top-right triangle up.

Helicopter

Follow these steps to enjoy making and playing with this whirring, flying helicopter.

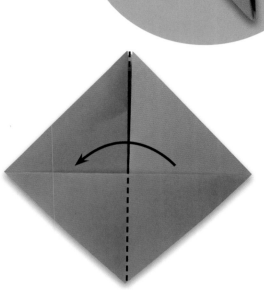

START WITH A SQUARE BASE

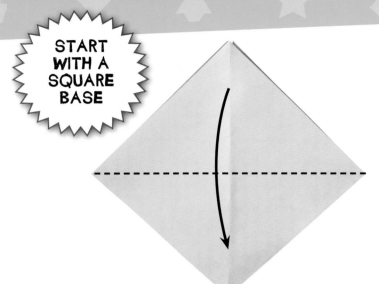

1 See how to make a square base on page 6. Turn so that the open part is at the top and the blue side is on the inside. Valley fold the top flap down to meet the bottom. Turn your model over and repeat on the reverse.

2 Valley fold the right flap over to the left, turn over and repeat on the reverse.

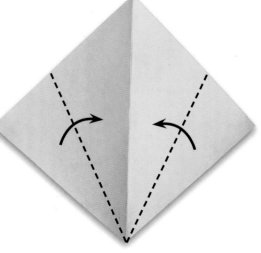

3 Valley fold the top-left and right flaps in to the middle.

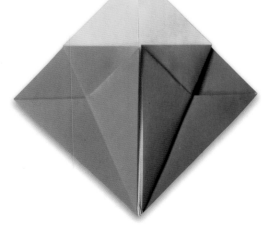

4 Your model should now look like this. Turn your paper over and repeat step 3 on the reverse.

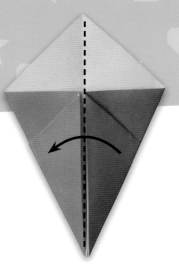

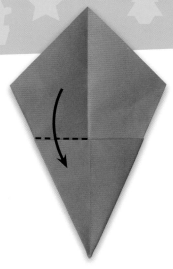

5 Valley fold the top right layer to the left. Turn your paper over and repeat on the reverse.

6 Your model should now look like this. Valley fold the top left section down to create your helicopter blades.

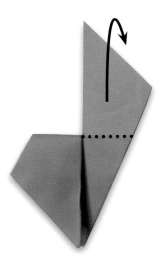

7 Mountain fold the top-right section down to create your second blade.

8
Use a paper clip to help weigh down the bottom of your helicopter. Drop it from somewhere high and watch it fly!

Holidays

Make your holidays extra special with these fun-filled origami projects. In this chapter, there are things to make for Christmas, Easter, Halloween, and Valentine's Day.

Easter bunny

Christmas tree

Spooky!

Halloween bat

Halloween pumpkin

Twinkle, twinkle!

Christmas star

Valentine's heart

Love!

151

Christmas wreath

At Christmas time, many people put wreaths on their front door. You could put your wreath on your bedroom door to get into the Christmas spirit.

1 Start with your paper white side up. Valley fold your paper in half from bottom to top, crease well, and then unfold.

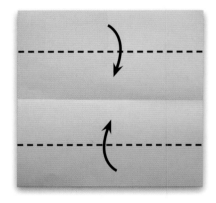

2 Valley fold the top and bottom sections into the middle.

3 Valley fold your paper in half upward so that the open side is at the top.

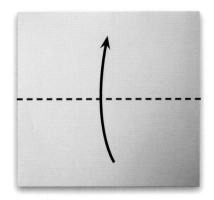

4 Valley fold down the left and right corners.

5 Valley fold your paper in half from right to left in the middle.

6 Your model should look like this. Repeat steps 1 to 5 on a new piece of paper 7 times so you have 8 pieces in total. Use green and red paper to make your wreath more festive.

Pocket 1

Pocket 2

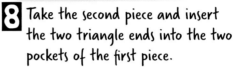

7 To put your wreath together, start with two pieces. Take the first piece, hold it by the triangle ends, and turn it so you can see the two pockets at the top.

Close-up of pockets.

8 Take the second piece and insert the two triangle ends into the two pockets of the first piece.

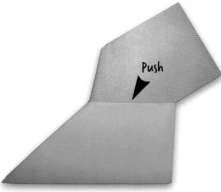

Push

9 Push the second piece in at an angle as far as it will go. Repeat this step with the third piece and so on.

Piece 8

Piece 1

10 To complete your model, insert the triangle ends of the first piece into the pockets of the eighth piece.

11 When your wreath is ready, you could decorate it by tying a lovely ribbon onto it.

Christmas star

This star can go at the very top of your Christmas tree. You could also make a few of them using different shades of paper to hang on your tree.

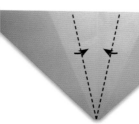

START WITH A WATERBOMB BASE

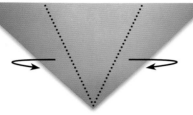

1 Find out how to make a waterbomb base on page 7. Place it with the point at the bottom. Mountain fold the top left and right flaps into the middle, crease, and unfold.

2 Valley fold the inner triangle sections of the top flaps, bringing the mountain folds you created in step 1 together into the middle.

3 Your model should look like this. Turn your paper over and repeat steps 1 and 2 on the reverse.

4 Valley fold the two top flaps down at the same time.

7 Turn over your star. It is now ready to be placed at the very top of the Christmas tree!

5 Your model should look like this. Press the middle down carefully to flatten it.

6 Your model should look like this.

Christmas tree

This little Christmas tree is perfect to place in your bedroom or on a desk to ensure you are in a festive mood!

START WITH A KITE BASE

1 Find out how to make a kite base on page 5. Place your kite base as shown.

2 Valley fold the top left and right sides into the middle.

3 Mountain fold the top point halfway down the white area.

4 Mountain fold across the middle.

7 Turn over your paper to see the finished tree. Stick some sequins on your tree to decorate it.

5 Turn your model over and around so that the point is at the top. Valley fold the top flap down to below the base of the triangle.

6 Your model should now look like this.

155

Winter icicle

Transform any room into a winter wonderland by making lots of these beautiful icicles.

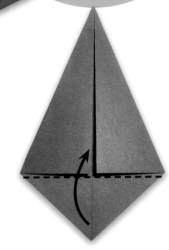

START WITH A SQUARE BASE

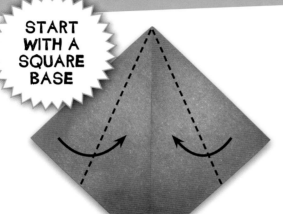

1 Find out how to make a square base on page 6. Turn so that the open end is facing downward. Valley fold the left and right sides into the middle.

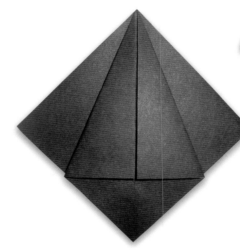

2 Turn your paper over and repeat step 1 on the reverse.

3 Your model should now look like this. Valley fold the top layer of the bottom flap up and crease well.

4 Turn your paper over and repeat step 3 on the reverse.

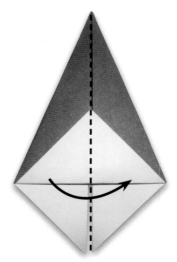

5 Valley fold the paper in the middle, crease well, and then unfold.

6 Take a second piece of paper and repeat steps 1 to 5 to create a second section.

7 Turn the second section so that the narrow end is pointing downward. Valley fold the top right flap over to the left.

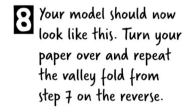

8 Your model should now look like this. Turn your paper over and repeat the valley fold from step 7 on the reverse.

Slot

Close-up of front and back sides.

Slot

Slot

Close-up of left and right sides.

Slot

Slot

Close-up of sections slotting together.

Slot

9 Slide your fingers inside each section to open them out a bit, then carefully slot the two sections together, tucking the blue and purple points behind the white triangles to hold the model in place.

10 Your icicle decoration is now ready. You could attach string to it and hang it on your Christmas tree, too!

Easter bunny

This little bunny makes a lovely decoration to celebrate Easter. All you need now is some chocolate to go with it!

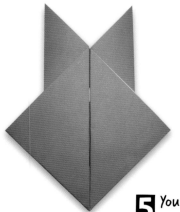

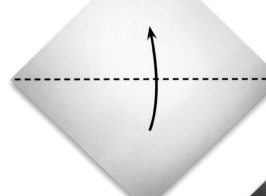

1 Place your paper as shown. Valley fold your paper diagonally.

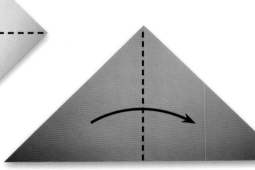

2 Valley fold your paper in the middle, crease well, and unfold.

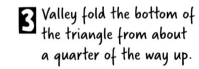

3 Valley fold the bottom of the triangle from about a quarter of the way up.

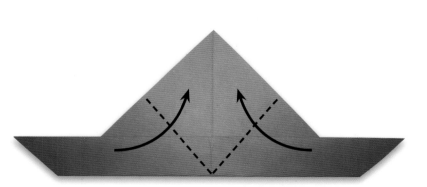

4 Valley fold the left and right points up into the middle.

5 Your model should look like this.

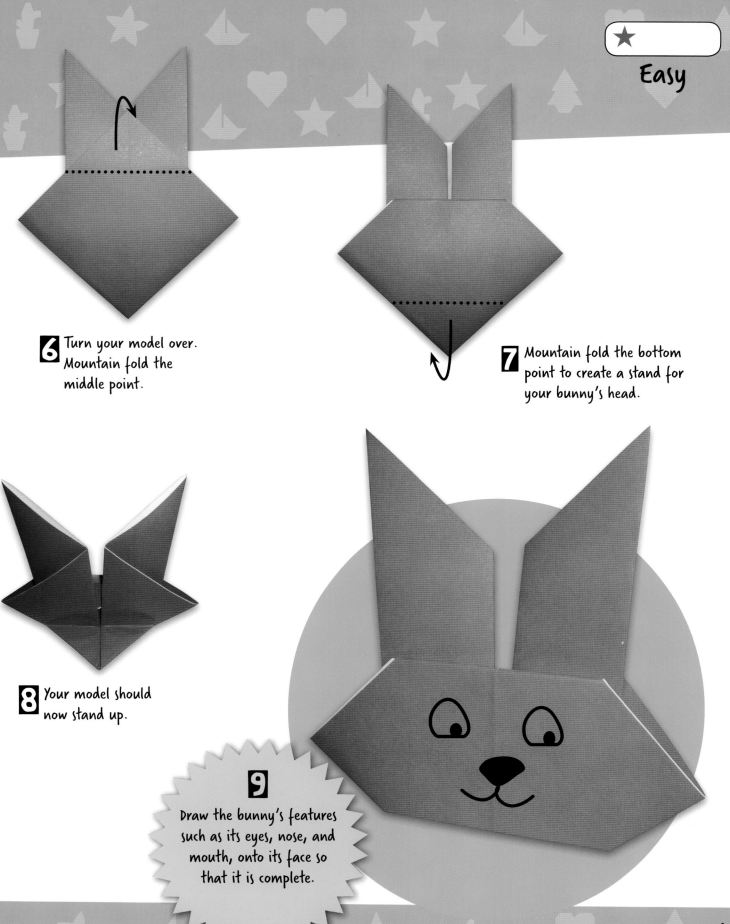

6 Turn your model over. Mountain fold the middle point.

7 Mountain fold the bottom point to create a stand for your bunny's head.

8 Your model should now stand up.

9

Draw the bunny's features such as its eyes, nose, and mouth, onto its face so that it is complete.

Halloween pumpkin

When it's Halloween, it's time for some spooky fun.
Start the festivities with this origami pumpkin.

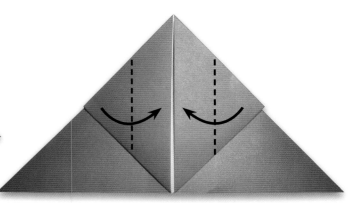

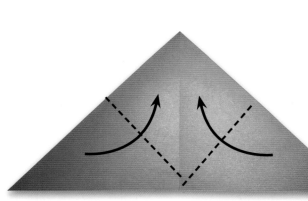

1 Find out how to make a waterbomb
base on page 7. Place your
waterbomb base with the point at
the top. Valley fold the top left and
right points up into the middle.

2 Valley fold the left and right
sides into the middle.

3 Valley fold the top points
down into the middle.

Slot

Close-up of pockets.

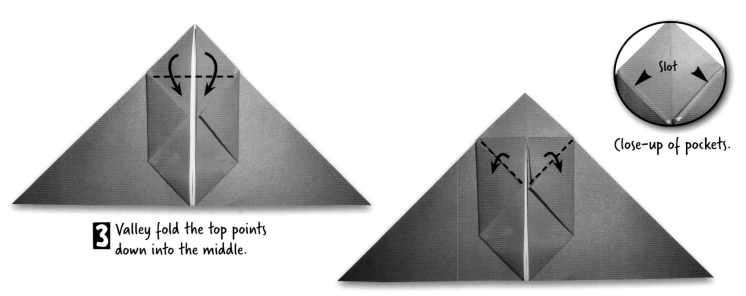

4 Valley fold the points and slot them into the
pockets of the side triangles.

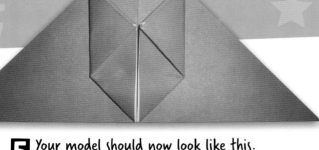

5 Your model should now look like this. Turn it over and repeat steps 1 to 5 on the reverse.

6 Valley fold the top left side over to the right.

7 Draw a scary face onto your pumpkin.

Hold here

Blow here

8 Your model should look something like this. Gently hold the top end of the pumpkin to cover the hole. You will find a small gap at the other end. Carefully blow into the gap. The pumpkin should start to inflate. If it does not inflate completely, use your fingers to gently pull out the sides.

9 Put your pumpkin on a window ledge to scare the trick-or-treaters. Do not put your pumpkin near candles!

Halloween bat

This spooky Halloween bat will scare all your friends and family into giving you treats on Halloween!

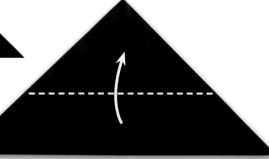

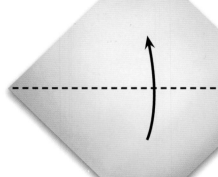

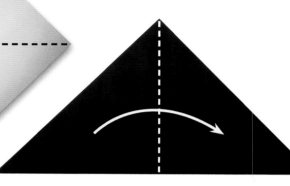

1 Place your paper as shown. Valley fold your paper diagonally and crease well.

2 Valley fold your paper in half from left to right. Crease well and unfold.

3 Valley fold your paper horizontally and crease well.

Close-up of head after fold.

4 Valley fold the top triangle down just above the front flap.

5 Valley fold the corners of the top section to shape your bat's head.

6 Mountain fold your paper in the middle and crease well.

162

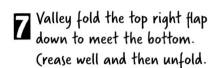

7 Valley fold the top right flap down to meet the bottom. Crease well and then unfold.

8 Valley fold the top flap up to create your bat's body. Crease well and then unfold.

9 Your model should now look like this. Turn your model over and repeat steps 7 and 8 on the reverse.

10 Now, open out your model so that it looks like this. Mountain fold the left and right sides to give shape to your bat's wings.

11 Your bat is ready. You could tie some string to it but be careful — you may find it hanging up-side-down where you least expect it!

Valentine's heart

This origami heart makes the perfect Valentine's Day gift for someone special.

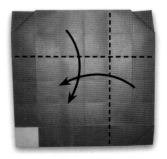

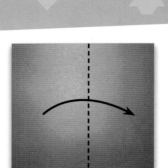

1 Place your paper as shown. Valley fold the paper in half, crease well, then unfold.

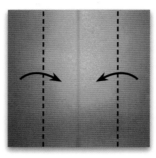

2 Valley fold the left and right sides into the middle. Crease well and then unfold.

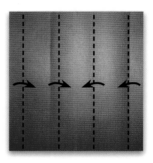

3 Valley fold the middle of each rectangle panel in turn. Crease well and then unfold.

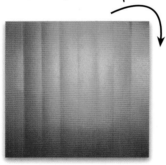

4 Rotate your paper 90 degrees and repeat steps 1 to 3.

5 Your paper will now be creased into lots of squares. Valley fold the top left corner diagonally so that it meets the second vertical crease.

6 Repeat the fold on the remaining three corners.

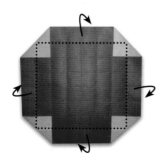

7 Mountain fold the outer folds to make your paper square again.

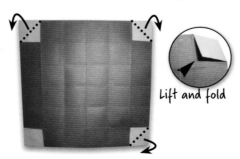

Lift and fold

8 Mountain fold three of the corners but, as you fold them, lift the white squares up and fold them back.

9 Valley fold the second horizontal fold from the top and the second vertical fo from the right. Crease well but leave op

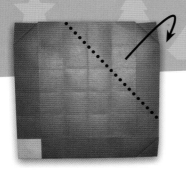

Press down

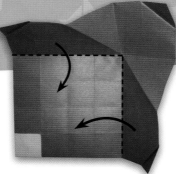

10 Now make a diagonal mountain fold in the top right corner where the two valley folds cross. Crease well but leave open.

11 You are now ready to collapse your paper. Valley fold the top and right sides and flatten your paper.

12 Your paper should now look like this. Press down to flatten the top right corner.

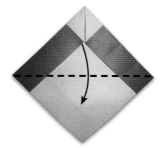

13 Now make a diagonal mountain fold in the top right corner where the two valley folds cross. Crease well but leave open.

14 You are now ready to collapse your paper. Valley fold the top and right sides and flatten your paper.

15 Your paper should now look like this. Press down to flatten the top right corner.

16 To finish your heart, flip it over so that it looks like this.

ORIGAMI FASHION

Tops

An easy way to change your outfit is to get a new top! Choose from long and hippy, fitted and pretty, short and flared, or simple and sporty. Take your pick to suit your mood!

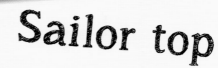

Sailor top

Ship ahoy!

Sports shirt

Anyone for tennis?

Crop top

Blouse

Smock top

Swing your thing!

Crop top

Fold this fun, short shirt and you can rock
a crop without ever needing to bare your belly!

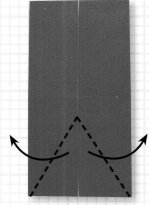

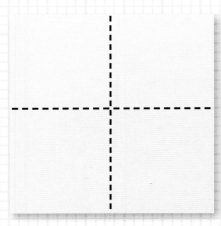

1 Fold the paper top to bottom
and unfold. Then left to right
and unfold.

2 Fold the edges in to meet the
central crease.

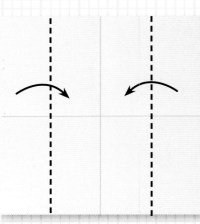

3 Make two angled folds from a
finger's width below the middle
to the bottom corners. These
will be the sleeves.

4
Valley fold the paper
at the top of the
angled folds you
just made.

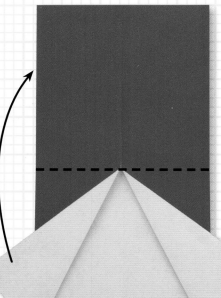

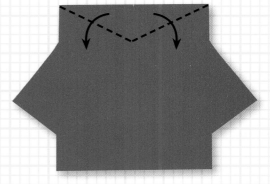

5 For the collar, make angled
creases from the top corners
to the middle of the paper.

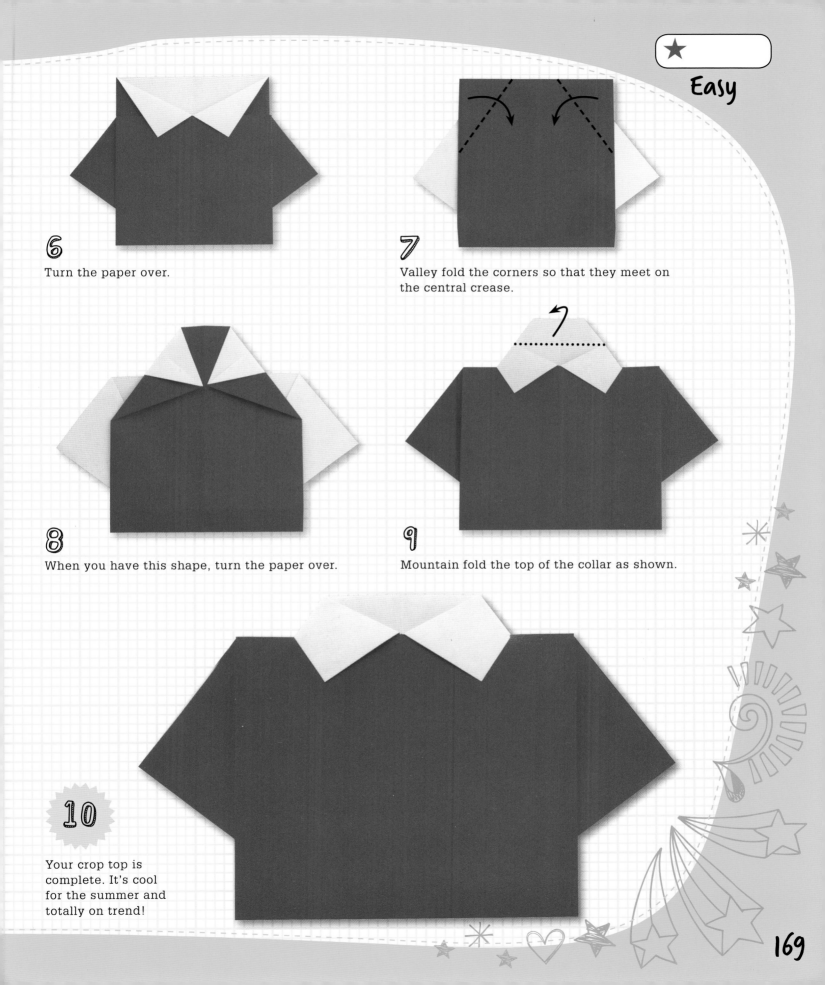

6
Turn the paper over.

7
Valley fold the corners so that they meet on the central crease.

8
When you have this shape, turn the paper over.

9
Mountain fold the top of the collar as shown.

10
Your crop top is complete. It's cool for the summer and totally on trend!

Sports shirt

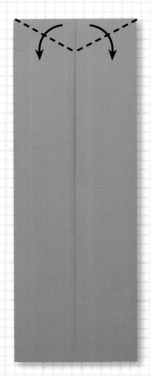

Get in training with this fab sports shirt.
Warm up with a few simple folds and creases and
before you know it, it'll be game, set, and match!

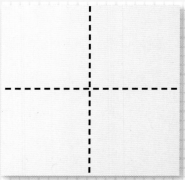

1 Fold the paper top to bottom and unfold. Then left to right and unfold.

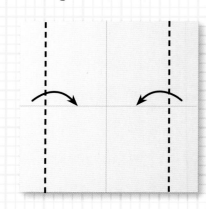

2 Fold in the sides 1 inch (25 mm) from either edge. Mark a faint line to help, if you like.

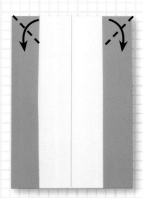

3 Valley fold the top corners to line up with the outside edges.

4 Fold in the edges to meet the central crease.

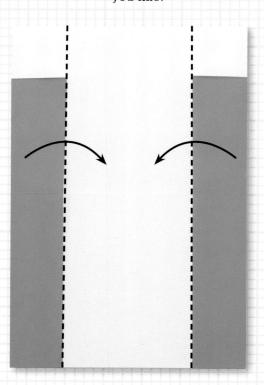

5 To make the collar, make two angled folds that meet in a "V" in the middle as shown.

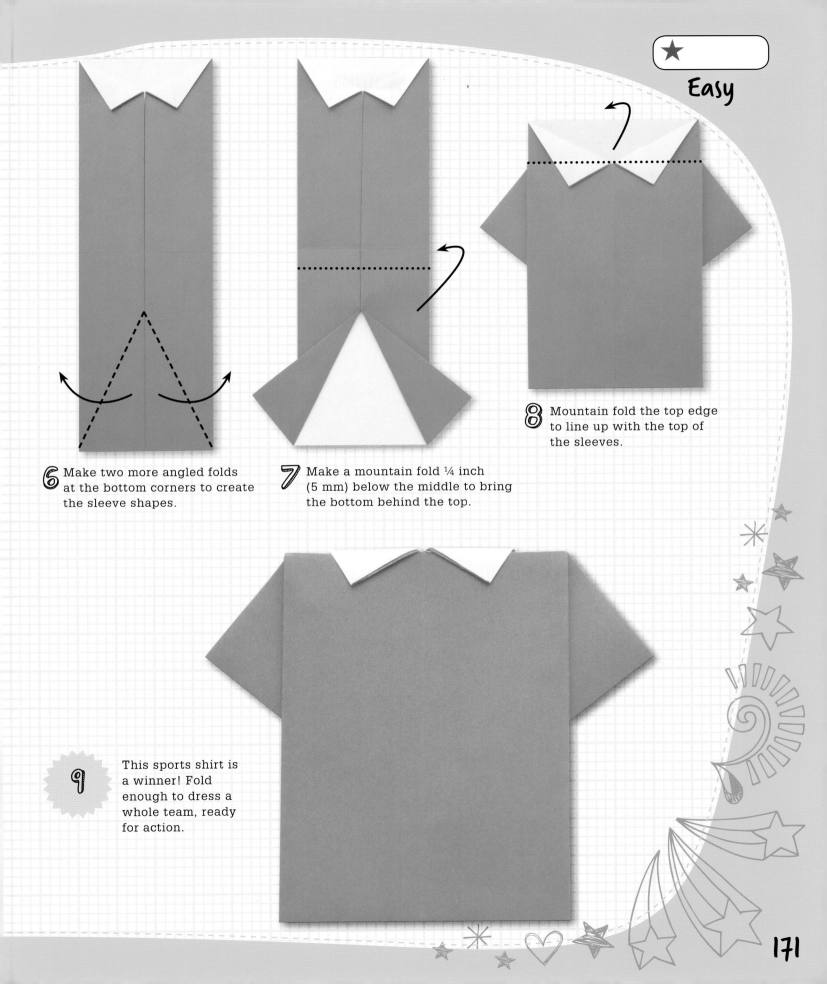

6 Make two more angled folds at the bottom corners to create the sleeve shapes.

7 Make a mountain fold ¼ inch (5 mm) below the middle to bring the bottom behind the top.

8 Mountain fold the top edge to line up with the top of the sleeves.

9 This sports shirt is a winner! Fold enough to dress a whole team, ready for action.

Smock top

Make a swinging smock top with plenty of Sixties style. Pick a strong shade to make the white neck and border really pop!

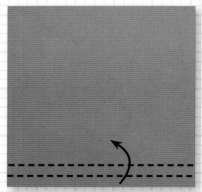

1 Make a valley fold ¼ inch (5 mm) from the bottom edge and fold it over twice to reveal a white strip.

2 Turn the paper over.

3 Make an angled crease on the left side around 2 inches (50 mm) from the edge at the top.

4
Fold back the corner as shown.

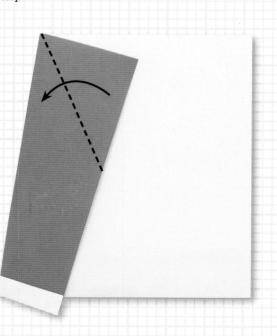

5 Now make an angled crease on the right side. Check that it matches the fold you made on the left side.

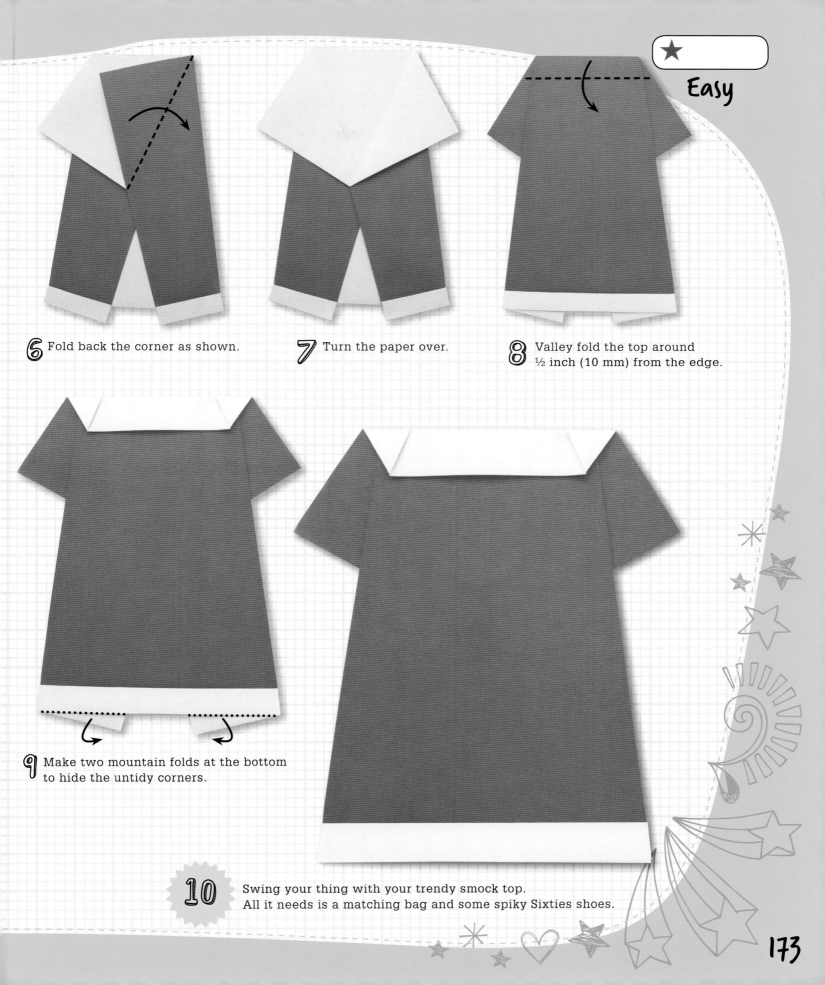

6 Fold back the corner as shown.

7 Turn the paper over.

8 Valley fold the top around ½ inch (10 mm) from the edge.

9 Make two mountain folds at the bottom to hide the untidy corners.

10 Swing your thing with your trendy smock top. All it needs is a matching bag and some spiky Sixties shoes.

173

Sailor top

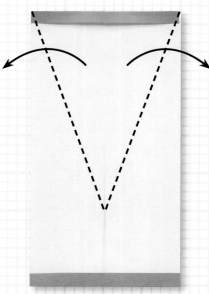

Ahoy there! This stylish boating top will add some fun to your paper fashions. Choose a bright ocean blue and set sail for the high seas!

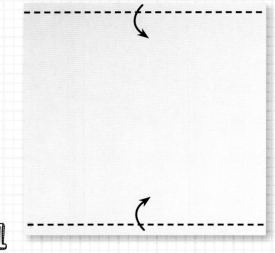

1 Valley fold a narrow section on the top and bottom edges.

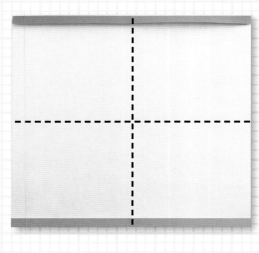

2 Fold the paper in half from top to bottom and unfold. Then fold it from left to right and unfold. Turn the paper over.

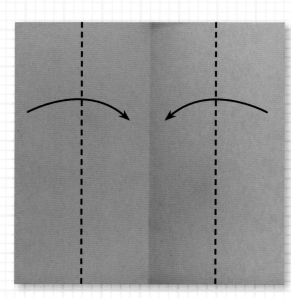

3 Fold the edges in to meet the central crease.

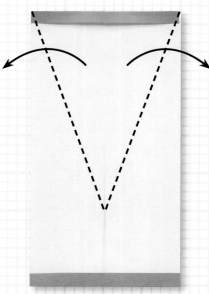

4 Make two angled folds from the top corners that meet in a "V" around 1½ inches (30 mm) below the middle. This will shape the sleeves and the collar.

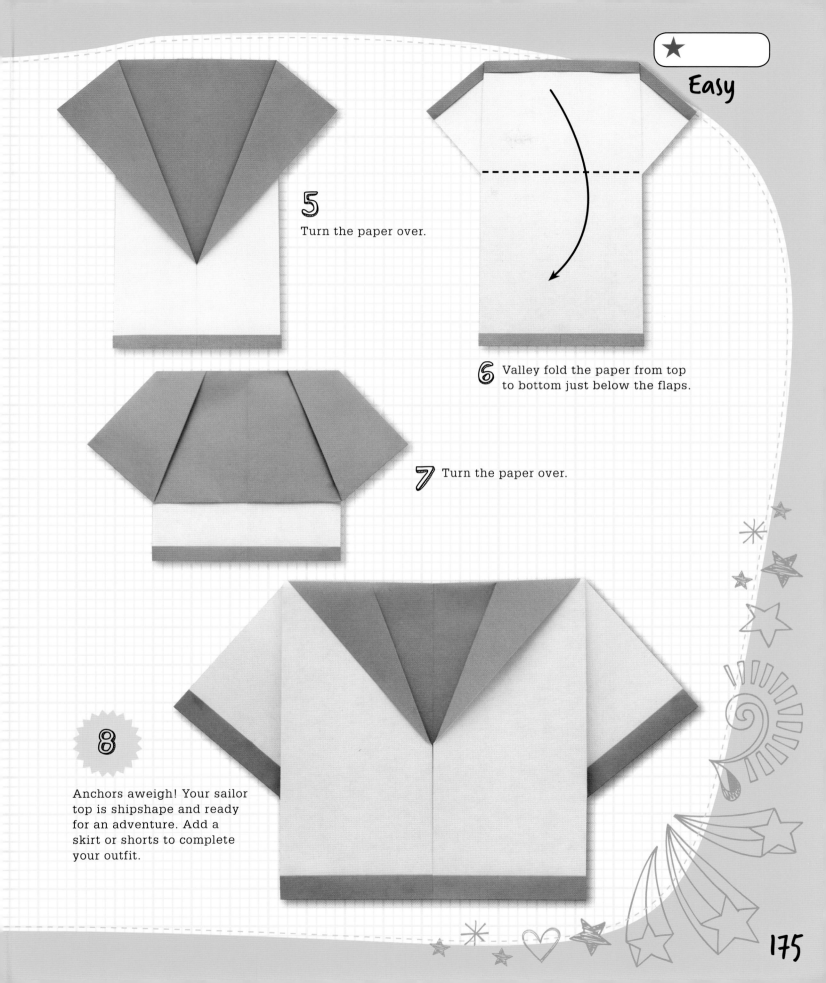

5 Turn the paper over.

6 Valley fold the paper from top to bottom just below the flaps.

7 Turn the paper over.

8 Anchors aweigh! Your sailor top is shipshape and ready for an adventure. Add a skirt or shorts to complete your outfit.

Blouse

Step out in style with this cute, short-sleeved blouse. Choose a pretty pink or pastel paper and follow the steps to fold a dainty collar and cuffs.

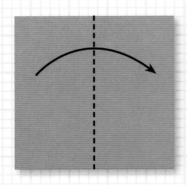

1 Fold the paper in half from left to right.

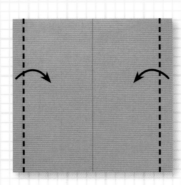

2 Fold in a ½ inch (10 mm) section on both edges.

3 Turn the paper over.

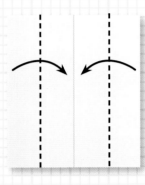

4 Fold the edges in to meet the central crease.

5 Make two angled creases as shown. When folded over, the edges should be straight.

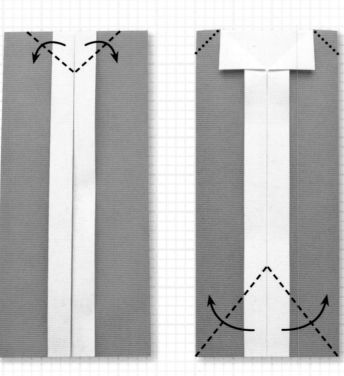

6 Shape the shoulders with mountain folds. Now make angled creases from the bottom corners.

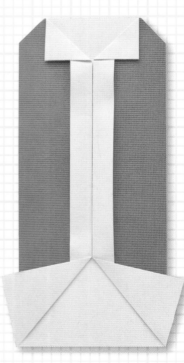

7 Turn the paper over.

9 Unfold the two white flaps.

10 Valley fold the sides as shown.

8 Valley fold the paper from bottom to top. The edge should meet the bottom of the corner folds.

11 Fold over these new flaps with two vertical creases from the bottom corners.

12 Fold down the upper flaps again along their original creases.

13 Turn the paper over to see the full effect.

14 One freshly folded blouse ready to wear! Pair it with a pleated skirt in a matching shade for a gorgeously girlie look.

177

Summer wear

Get ready for the summer with a cool collection of outfits. There's something for every sunny occasion, from picnics to pool parties!

T-shirt

Summer dress

Let's have a barbecue!

Shorts

Swimsuit

Fancy a dip?

Skater dress

I've packed a picnic!

Pleated skirt

179

T-shirt and shorts

Fold a pair of easy shorts and a comfy T-shirt. It's the perfect outfit for hot summer days. Coordinate the top and shorts, or mix and match different papers.

T-SHIRT

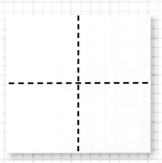

1 Fold the paper from left to right and unfold. Then fold it top to bottom and unfold.

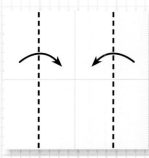

2 Fold in the edges to meet the central crease.

3 Valley fold a narrow section on both edges so a white strip is showing.

4 Make the sleeves with two angled creases from the middle of the inside edges to the bottom corners.

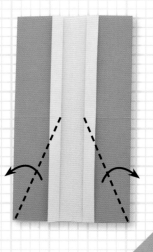

5 Valley fold the paper in half from the bottom to the top. Now your T-shirt is nearly finished.

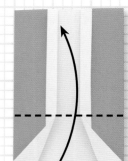

6 Turn the paper over and press down firmly on the creases. Your crisp, new T-shirt is ready for the next sunny day!

SHORTS

1 Follow steps 1 and 2 for T-shirt, then unfold the paper. Fold the bottom edge in, as shown.

2 Turn the paper over.

3 Make angled creases from the bottom corners to the first crease along the top edge on either side.

4 Fold in one side, pressing down firmly. Repeat on the other side. These will be the legs.

5 Mountain fold the top half of the paper behind the bottom half.

6 Check that the folded half does not show below the white strip. Make a crease ½ inch (10 mm) from the top edge.

7 Fold down along the new crease and press firmly to make the waistband. Your shorts are finished!

8 Now team your shorts up with your T-shirt. What could be cooler on a hot summer day?

Swimsuit

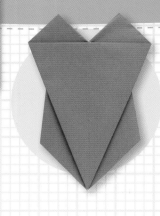

Make a splash on sunny days with a cute swimsuit that's easy to fold. Blend in at the beach with ocean blue, or stand out at the pool with a zingy shade.

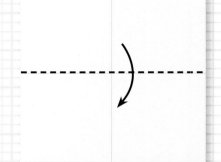

1 Fold the paper in half from top to bottom and unfold. Then from left to right and unfold.

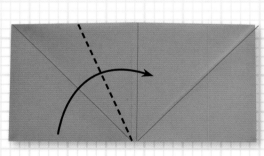

2 Fold the paper in half from top to bottom once more.

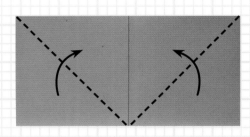

3 Fold the bottom corners up to meet in the middle of the top edge.

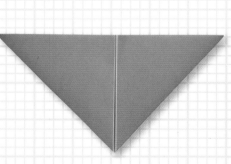

4 You should now have a triangle. Unfold the last two folds.

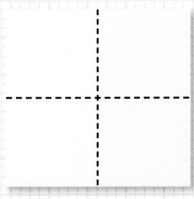

5 Fold the left side over so the bottom edge meets the diagonal crease on the opposite side.

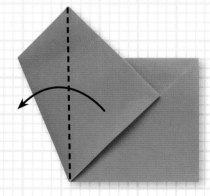

6 Valley fold the paper along the original fold to make a triangle.

7 Repeat steps 5 and 6 on the other side. You can open out the paper to check that the bottom edge meets the diagonal crease on the opposite side.

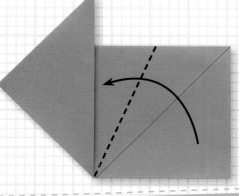

8 You should have two triangles that meet to form a square. Make two angled creases at the top.

9 Fold down, making sure the bottom edges are straight and the outer edges line up, then unfold.

10 Valley fold the left side from the edge of the crease, as shown.

11 Repeat on the right side.

12 Your paper should look like this. Turn the paper over.

13 Mountain fold the top corners along the creases that you made before. Press down firmly.

14 Your strapless swimsuit is ready for a dip. Time to grab the sunscreen and hit the beach!

Pleated skirt

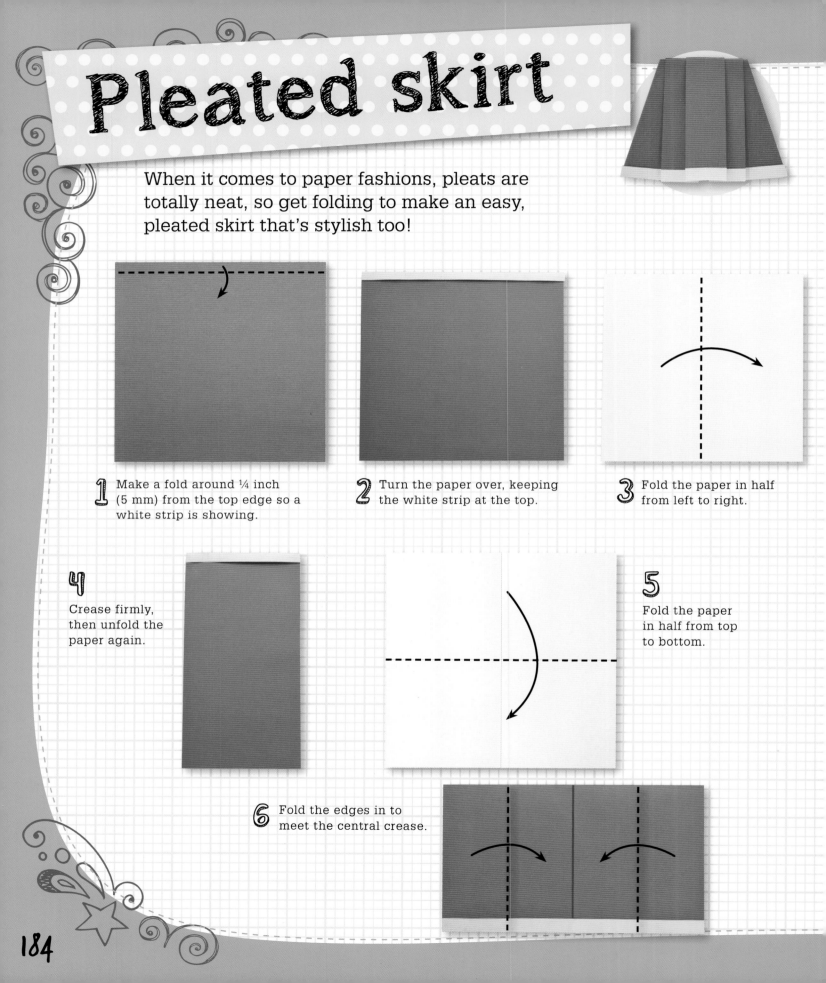

When it comes to paper fashions, pleats are totally neat, so get folding to make an easy, pleated skirt that's stylish too!

1 Make a fold around ¼ inch (5 mm) from the top edge so a white strip is showing.

2 Turn the paper over, keeping the white strip at the top.

3 Fold the paper in half from left to right.

4 Crease firmly, then unfold the paper again.

5 Fold the paper in half from top to bottom.

6 Fold the edges in to meet the central crease.

7 Repeat step 6, folding the edges in to meet the central crease.

8 Your paper should look like this. Unfold the paper, keeping the white strip at the bottom.

9 Turn the paper over.

10 Now make the first pleat. Take the third crease from the left to meet the central crease. Press it flat.

11 Repeat step 10 on the other side, taking the third crease from the right to meet the central crease. Press it flat.

12 You should now have a pleat down the middle of the paper.

It should look like this from the side. Turn the paper over.

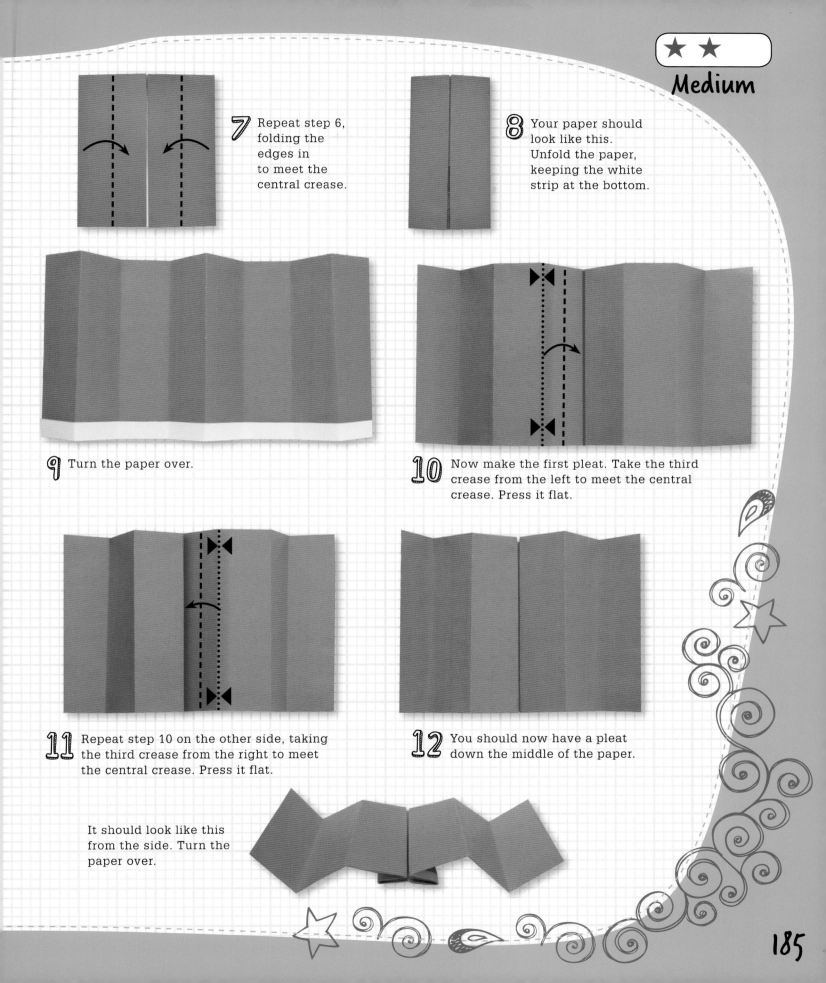

Pleated skirt

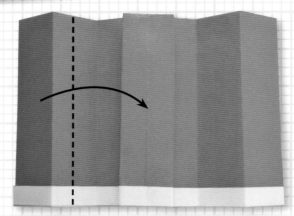

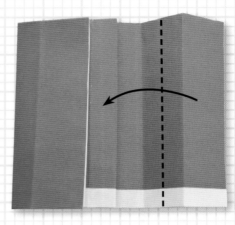

13 With the white strip along the bottom, fold the left edge in to meet the central crease.

14 Then fold the right edge in to meet the central crease.

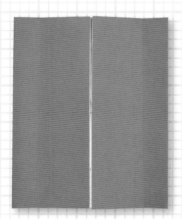

15 Unfold both sides, making sure that the pleat you made is still in place.

16 Turn the paper over, keeping the white strip at the bottom.

17

Now make another pleat. Take the second crease from the left and fold it over along the third crease.

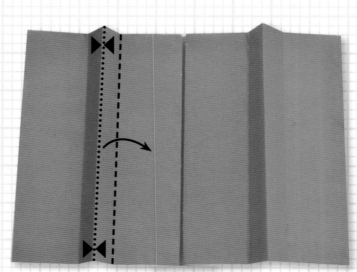

18 Repeat step 17 on the other side, taking the second crease from the right and folding it over along the third crease.

19 Make a valley fold from the first crease on the top edge to the bottom corner.

20 Make a matching fold on the other side to create the flared shape of the skirt.

21 Fold down the top ½ inch (10 mm) of the skirt to hide the open edges. Your skirt is nearly ready.

22 Press down firmly along the top to crease the pleated layers, then turn the paper over.

23 Ta-da! One neatly pleated skirt, complete with a pretty band, ready to swing into action!

Summer dress

It takes just a few minutes of folding to create this fabulous, bright summer dress. Use different papers to create a whole summer wardrobe.

1 Fold the paper left to right and unfold. Then fold it top to bottom and unfold.

2 Make a valley crease in the bottom half of the paper.

3 Fold the bottom edge of the paper up to the central crease, then unfold.

4 Make another crease halfway between the bottom of the paper and the valley crease.

5 Fold the bottom of the paper up to the new crease, so a section of white is showing.

6 Turn the paper over and fold the edges in to meet the central crease.

7 Make a step fold halfway between the top and the white strip at the bottom.

8 Press down on the step fold so it lies flat. Turn the paper over.

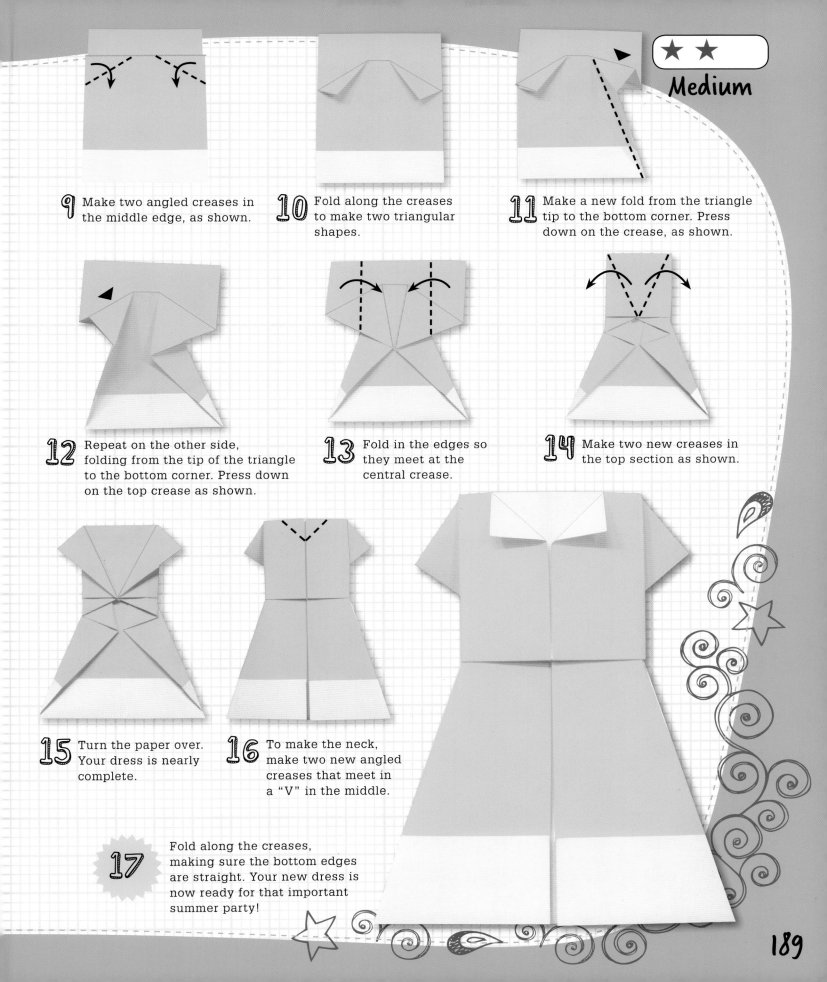

9 Make two angled creases in the middle edge, as shown.

10 Fold along the creases to make two triangular shapes.

11 Make a new fold from the triangle tip to the bottom corner. Press down on the crease, as shown.

12 Repeat on the other side, folding from the tip of the triangle to the bottom corner. Press down on the top crease as shown.

13 Fold in the edges so they meet at the central crease.

14 Make two new creases in the top section as shown.

15 Turn the paper over. Your dress is nearly complete.

16 To make the neck, make two new angled creases that meet in a "V" in the middle.

17 Fold along the creases, making sure the bottom edges are straight. Your new dress is now ready for that important summer party!

Skater dress

This pretty, everyday skater dress is a must-have for every girl's summer wardrobe. Fold these neat pleats and give it a twirl!

1 Fold the paper in half from top to bottom and unfold. Then from left to right and unfold.

2 Fold the edges in to meet the central crease.

3 Unfold the paper.

4 Fold in both sides about ½ inch (10 mm) from the edge.

5 Mountain fold the sides along the creases that you made earlier.

6 Make a new crease about 1 inch (25 mm) from the top edge.

7 Fold down the paper and crease firmly.

190

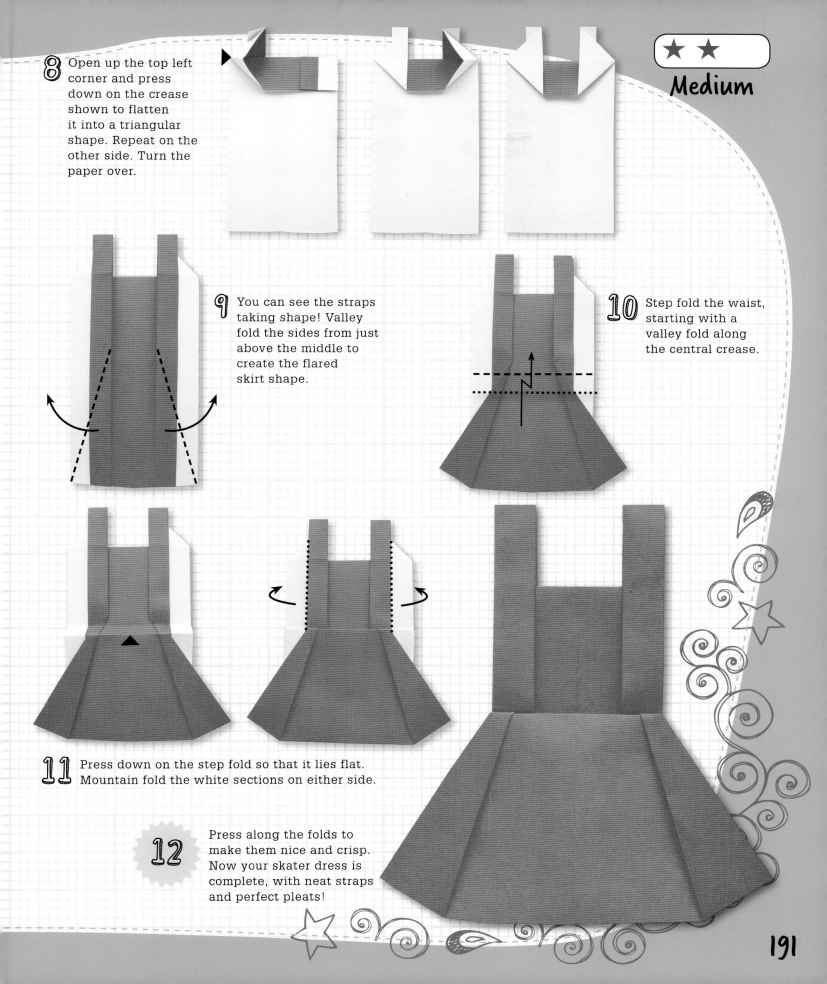

8 Open up the top left corner and press down on the crease shown to flatten it into a triangular shape. Repeat on the other side. Turn the paper over.

9 You can see the straps taking shape! Valley fold the sides from just above the middle to create the flared skirt shape.

10 Step fold the waist, starting with a valley fold along the central crease.

11 Press down on the step fold so that it lies flat. Mountain fold the white sections on either side.

12 Press along the folds to make them nice and crisp. Now your skater dress is complete, with neat straps and perfect pleats!

Dressing up

This collection really is super-stylish! Fold some fabulous evening wear for glittering parties and glamorous dinner dates.

Let's dance!

Party dress

Evening gown

Kick up your heels!

May I take your coat?

Dress coat

Smart suit

High heels

193

Smart suit

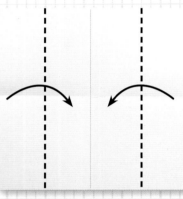

Make your creases extra sharp and your folds totally faultless for this snappy two-piece suit.

PART 1

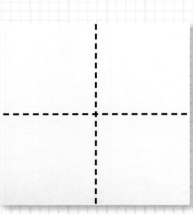

1 Fold the paper in half from top to bottom and unfold. Then from left to right and unfold.

2 Mountain fold a narrow strip on the top edge. This will be the sleeve cuffs.

3 Fold the edges in to meet the central crease.

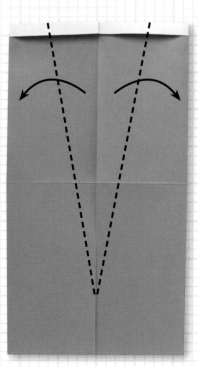

4 Make two angled creases that meet in a "V" as shown. When folded back, the tips of the flaps should meet the edges of the paper.

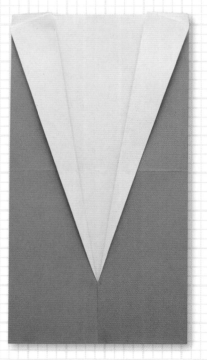

5 Turn the paper over.

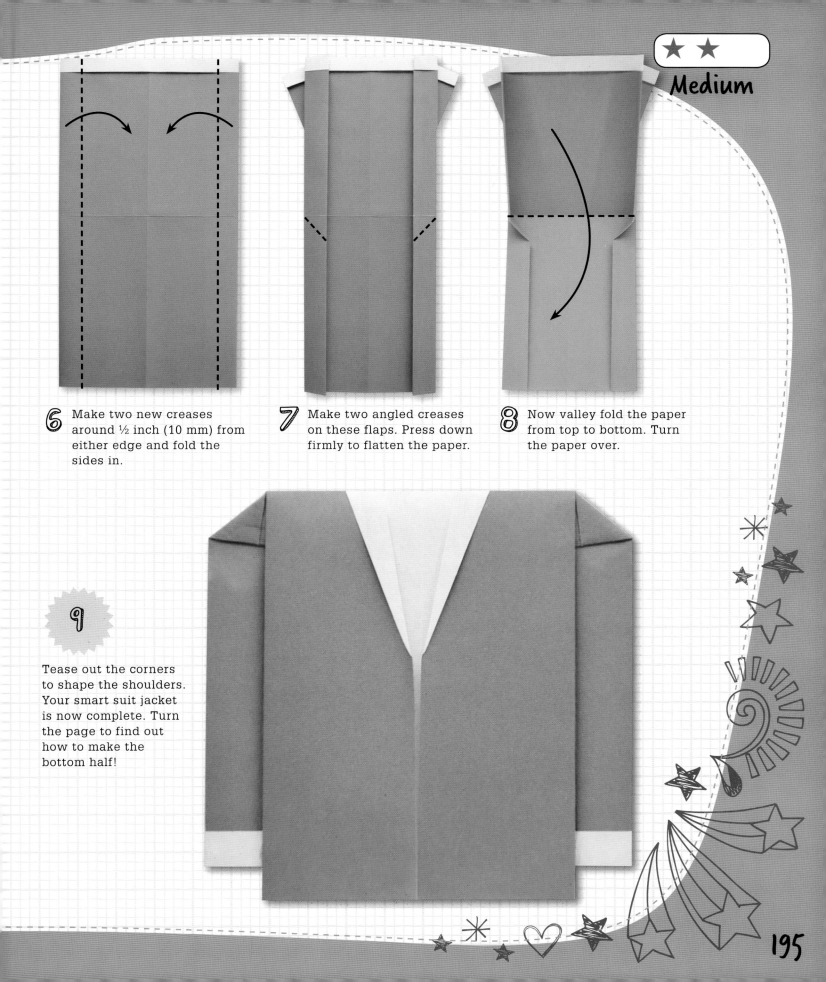

6 Make two new creases around ½ inch (10 mm) from either edge and fold the sides in.

7 Make two angled creases on these flaps. Press down firmly to flatten the paper.

8 Now valley fold the paper from top to bottom. Turn the paper over.

9 Tease out the corners to shape the shoulders. Your smart suit jacket is now complete. Turn the page to find out how to make the bottom half!

Smart suit

PART 2

1 Fold the paper from top to bottom and unfold. Then from left to right and unfold.

2 Fold the edges in to meet the central crease.

3 Unfold the paper.

4 Fold in the side with a slightly angled crease as shown.

5 Repeat on the other side.

6 Mountain fold the edges at the same slight angle.

7 Mountain fold the top as shown.

8 Now the two parts of your suit are pressed and ready. Put them together and you have one stylish outfit all set for a dinner date!

High heels

What could be more elegant than a brand new pair of high heels? Fold these right and they'll stand up on their own.

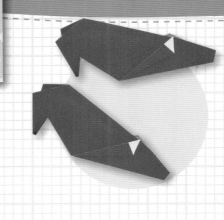

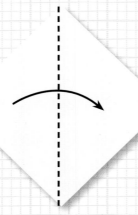

1. Place the paper as shown. Make a crease down the middle, then unfold.

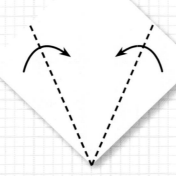

2. Make two diagonal creases from halfway along the top edges to the bottom middle.

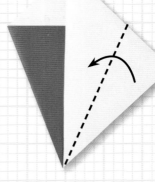

3. Fold in one side, making sure the top edge is straight. Repeat on the other side.

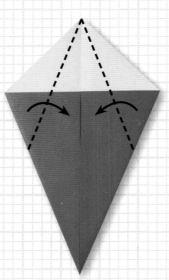

4. Make two new creases as shown by folding in the side points to the central crease.

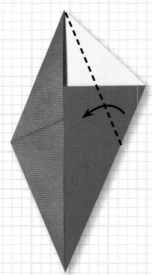

5. Fold one side into the central crease to make a triangle shape. Repeat on the other side.

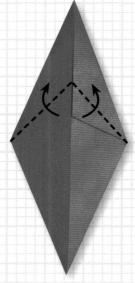

6. Make two new creases in the triangles you have just made. Line up with the outside edges.

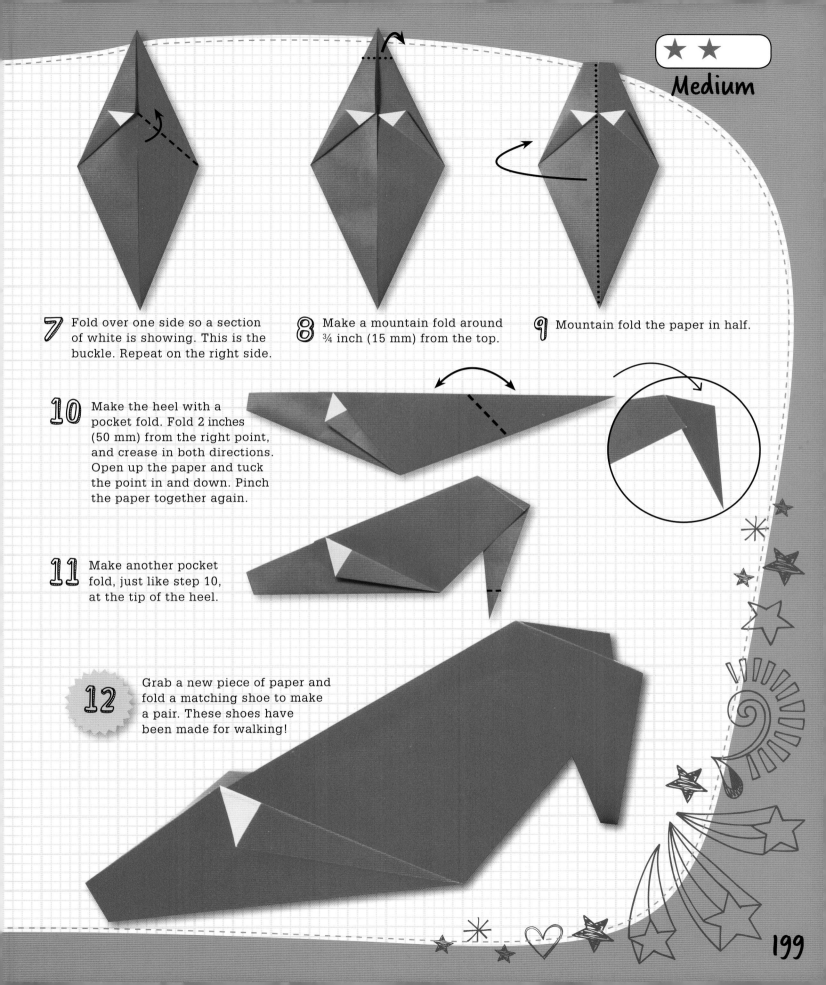

7 Fold over one side so a section of white is showing. This is the buckle. Repeat on the right side.

8 Make a mountain fold around ¾ inch (15 mm) from the top.

9 Mountain fold the paper in half.

10 Make the heel with a pocket fold. Fold 2 inches (50 mm) from the right point, and crease in both directions. Open up the paper and tuck the point in and down. Pinch the paper together again.

11 Make another pocket fold, just like step 10, at the tip of the heel.

12 Grab a new piece of paper and fold a matching shoe to make a pair. These shoes have been made for walking!

Dress coat

Fold this classy coat to wear over a party dress or a long evening gown. It's the perfect way to keep out the cold during chilly nights on the town.

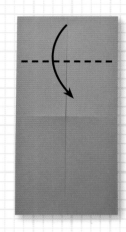

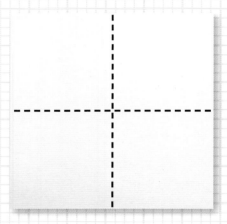

1 Fold the paper from top to bottom and unfold. Then from left to right and unfold.

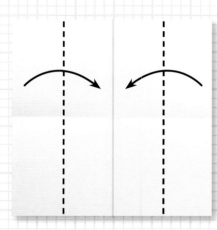

2 Fold in the edges to meet the central crease.

3 Now fold down the top edge to meet the central crease.

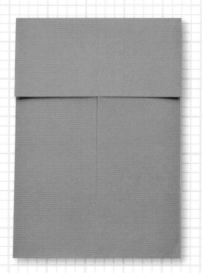

4 Turn the paper over.

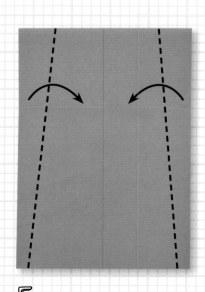

5 Make an angled crease on either side and fold in the edges.

6 Hold down the lower part of the left-hand flap with your finger and open up the top corner.

7

Press down on the crease on the top edge and flatten the paper to make a triangular shape. This is a sleeve and collar!

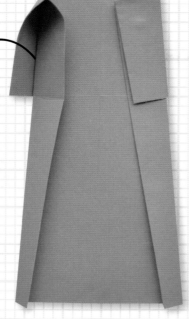

8

Repeat on the other side. Try to make the points of the collar match.

9

Mountain fold a narrow strip along the edges of the sleeves.

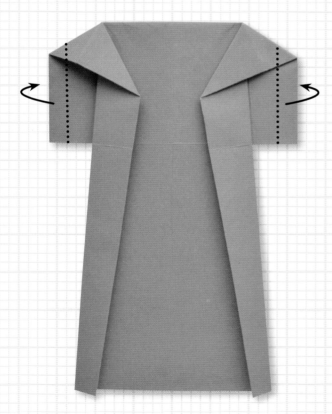

10

Your stylish new coat is ready. Don't forget your party invitation on your way out the door. TAXI!

Party dress

Finding the perfect dress for a party couldn't be easier! With its tiny waist and full, swishing skirt, this one is sure to be a hit on the dance floor.

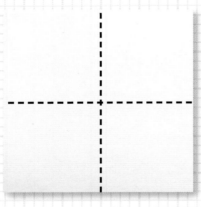

1 Fold the paper from top to bottom and unfold. Then from left to right and unfold.

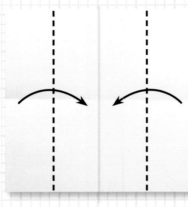

2 Fold in the edges to meet the central crease.

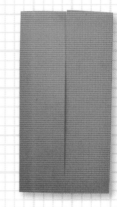

3 Open out the paper and turn it over.

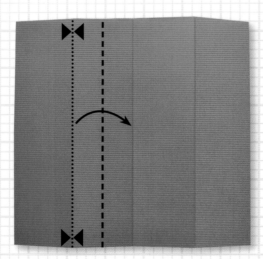

4 Now make a pleat. Take the crease on the left to meet the central crease.

5 Press flat to crease the paper underneath.

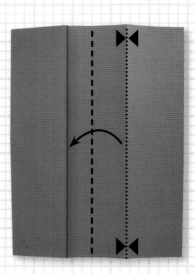

6 Repeat on the other side, taking the crease on the right to meet the central crease. Press flat.

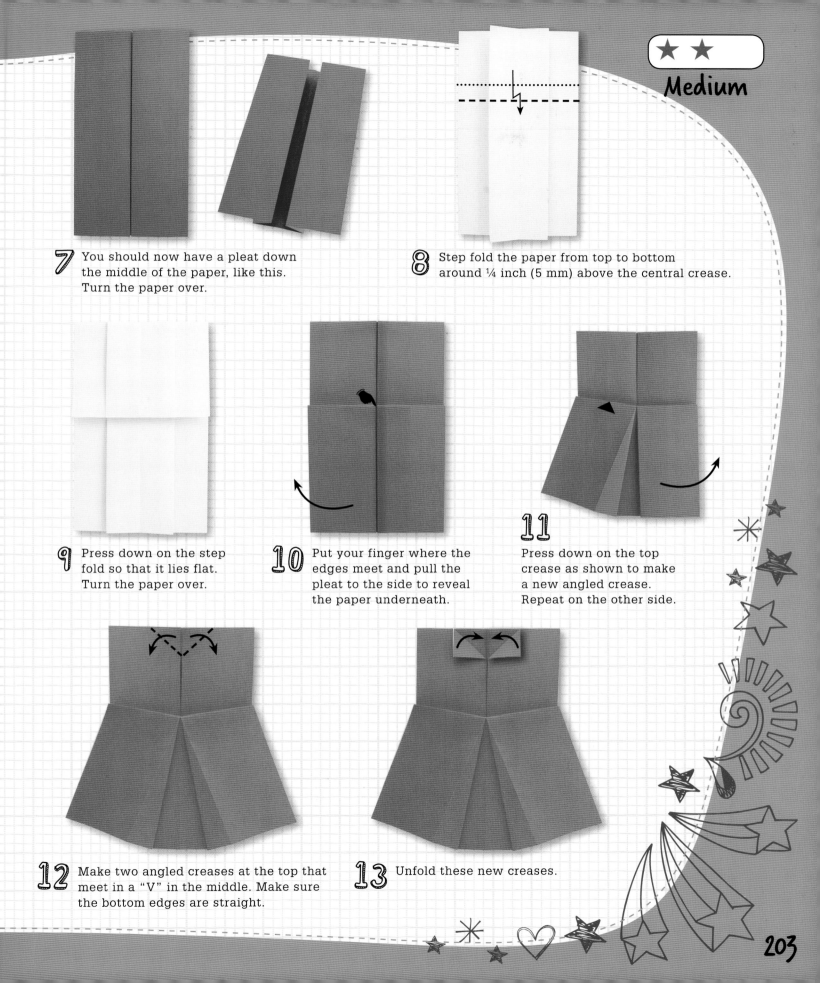

7 You should now have a pleat down the middle of the paper, like this. Turn the paper over.

8 Step fold the paper from top to bottom around ¼ inch (5 mm) above the central crease.

9 Press down on the step fold so that it lies flat. Turn the paper over.

10 Put your finger where the edges meet and pull the pleat to the side to reveal the paper underneath.

11 Press down on the top crease as shown to make a new angled crease. Repeat on the other side.

12 Make two angled creases at the top that meet in a "V" in the middle. Make sure the bottom edges are straight.

13 Unfold these new creases.

Party dress

14 Turn the paper over.

15 Make a valley fold ¾ inch (15 mm) from the top edge.

16 Unfold the new crease.

17 Open up the pleat and place your finger on it. Press down on the crease as shown. Flatten the paper to make a triangular shape. Repeat on the other side.

18 Valley fold the left side on the upper section as shown.

19 The lower section will be pulled across. Press down on it to make an angled crease. This creates the flared shape of the skirt.

20
Repeat on the other side, folding in the upper section and making an angled crease on the lower section.

21 Valley fold the upper sections from the outer to the inner corners to make the sleeves.

22 Turn the paper over to see the finished dress.

23
This frock is ready to rock! It's perfect for twirling the night away or sitting prettily on the side.

Evening gown

This dazzling evening gown is made for glittering balls and glamorous parties. Choose midnight blue or deep purple for a totally elegant look.

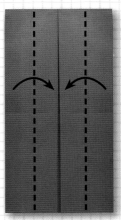

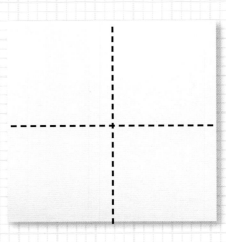

1 Fold the paper from top to bottom and unfold. Then from left to right and unfold.

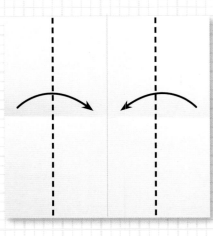

2 Fold the edges in to meet the central crease.

3 Fold the edges in again to meet the central crease.

4 Completely unfold the paper. Turn the paper over.

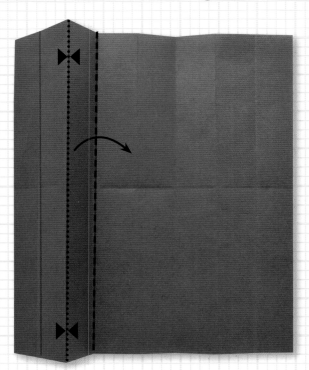

5 Now make a pleat. Take the second crease from the left to meet the central crease. Fold flat.

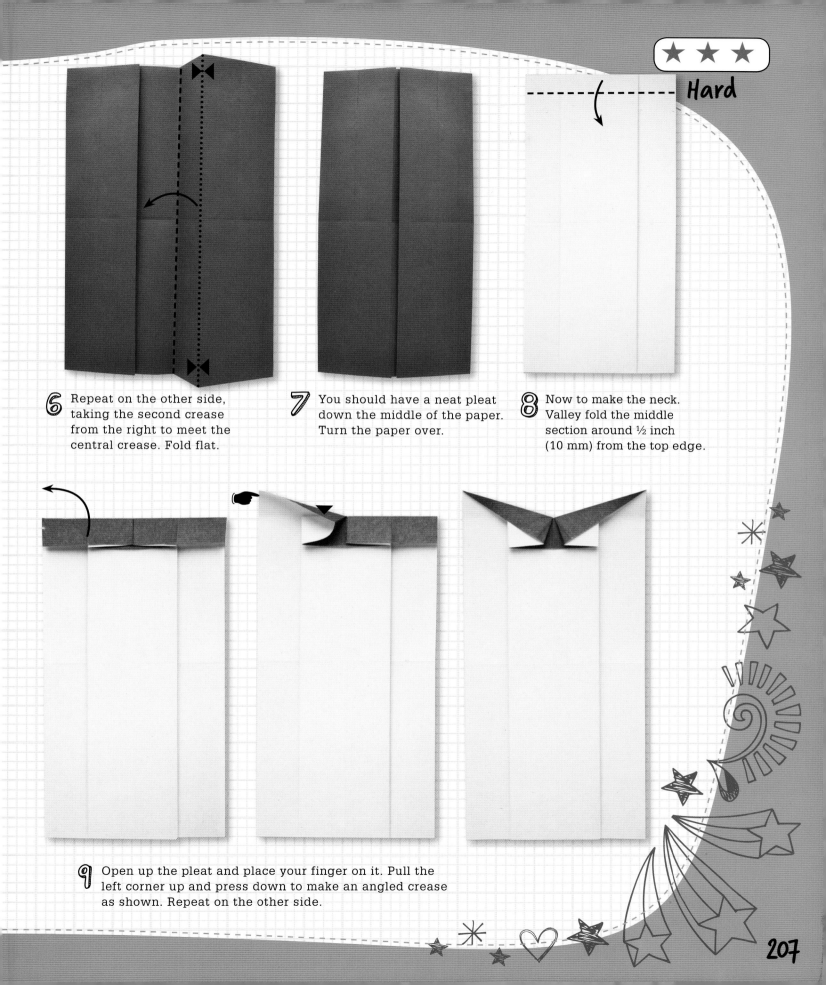

6 Repeat on the other side, taking the second crease from the right to meet the central crease. Fold flat.

7 You should have a neat pleat down the middle of the paper. Turn the paper over.

8 Now to make the neck. Valley fold the middle section around ½ inch (10 mm) from the top edge.

9 Open up the pleat and place your finger on it. Pull the left corner up and press down to make an angled crease as shown. Repeat on the other side.

207

Evening gown

10

Fold in the left and right edges to meet the central crease.

11

Make angled creases from the middle to the bottom corners. This is the skirt.

12

Create the waist with a step fold across the middle of the paper.

13

Press down on the step fold so that it lies flat.

14

Now to shape the waist. First make an angled crease on the upper section.

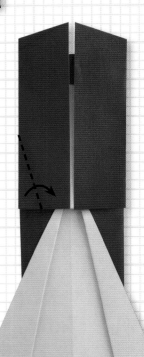

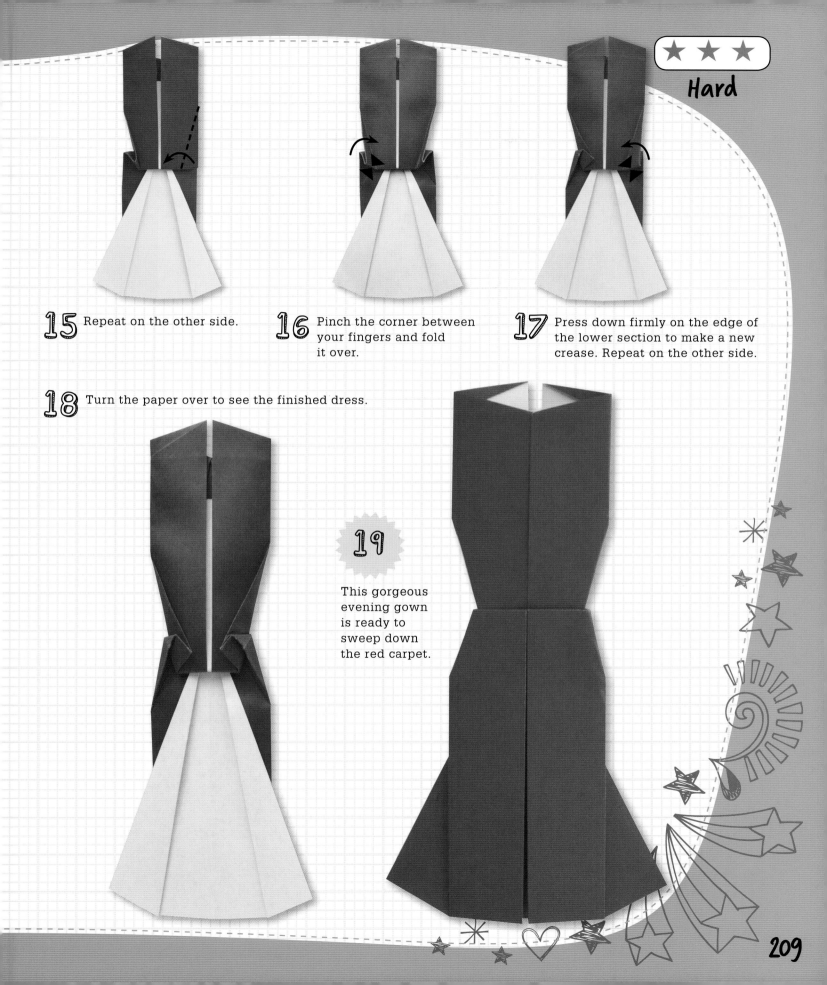

15 Repeat on the other side.

16 Pinch the corner between your fingers and fold it over.

17 Press down firmly on the edge of the lower section to make a new crease. Repeat on the other side.

18 Turn the paper over to see the finished dress.

19

This gorgeous evening gown is ready to sweep down the red carpet.

Accessories

Pick the perfect accessories to match your paper outfits, whatever the weather. There are cool shades and warm mittens, boots, bags, and even some paper bling!

Clutch bag

Necktie

Hey, dude!

Sunglasses

Mittens

Socks

Let it snow!

Bangle

Nice boots!

Boots

Necktie

There are no tricky knots to master with this origami necktie. Follow the simple steps and you will have a fantastic result in minutes!

1

Place the paper as shown. Fold it in half from left to right and unfold.

2

Fold in the left and right edges from the top corner to meet the central crease.

3

Now you have a kite shape. Turn the paper over.

4

Valley fold the top so that the point lines up with the points on either side.

5

Fold up the tip as shown.

6

Make a crease just above the tip and fold the paper up once more.

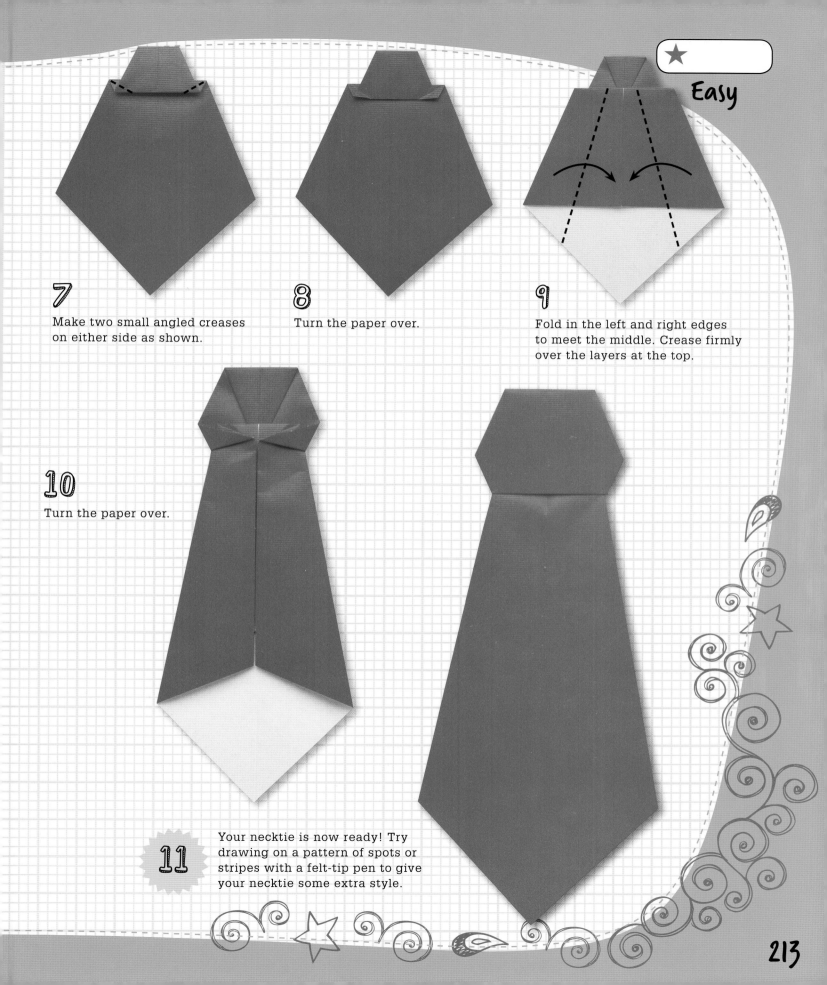

7

Make two small angled creases on either side as shown.

8

Turn the paper over.

9

Fold in the left and right edges to meet the middle. Crease firmly over the layers at the top.

10

Turn the paper over.

11

Your necktie is now ready! Try drawing on a pattern of spots or stripes with a felt-tip pen to give your necktie some extra style.

Sunglasses

Keep your cool with these designer sunglasses. It only takes a few easy folds and a lot of rolls to create these trendy wrap-around shades.

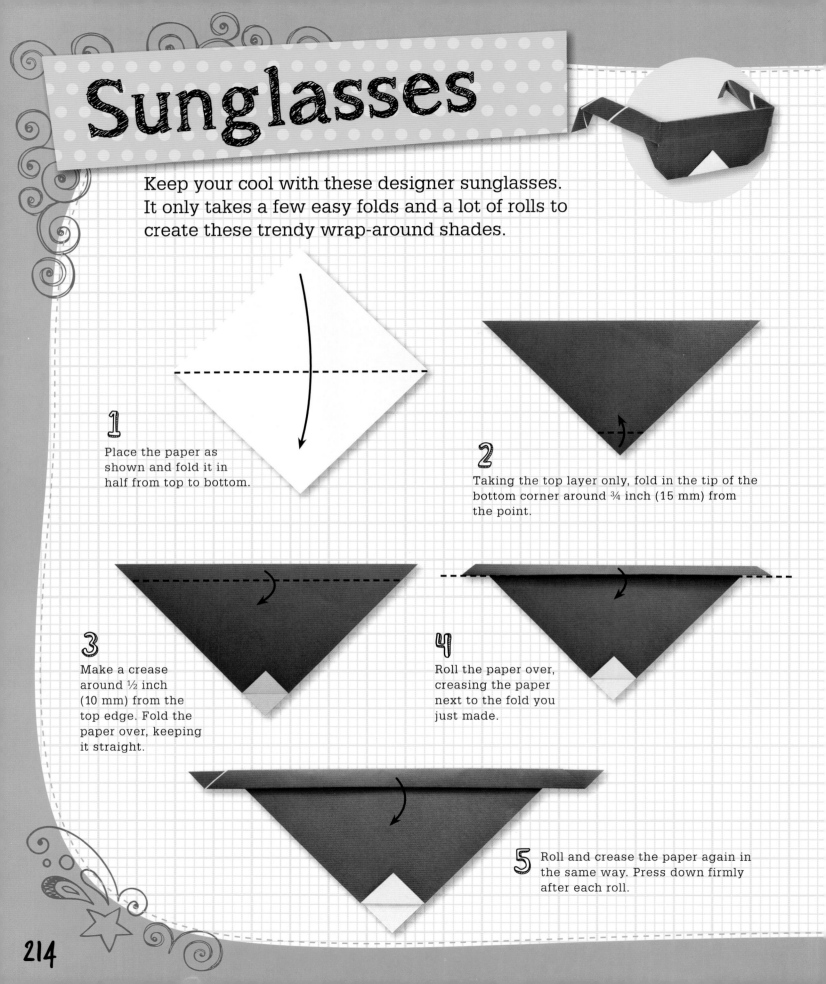

1 Place the paper as shown and fold it in half from top to bottom.

2 Taking the top layer only, fold in the tip of the bottom corner around ¾ inch (15 mm) from the point.

3 Make a crease around ½ inch (10 mm) from the top edge. Fold the paper over, keeping it straight.

4 Roll the paper over, creasing the paper next to the fold you just made.

5 Roll and crease the paper again in the same way. Press down firmly after each roll.

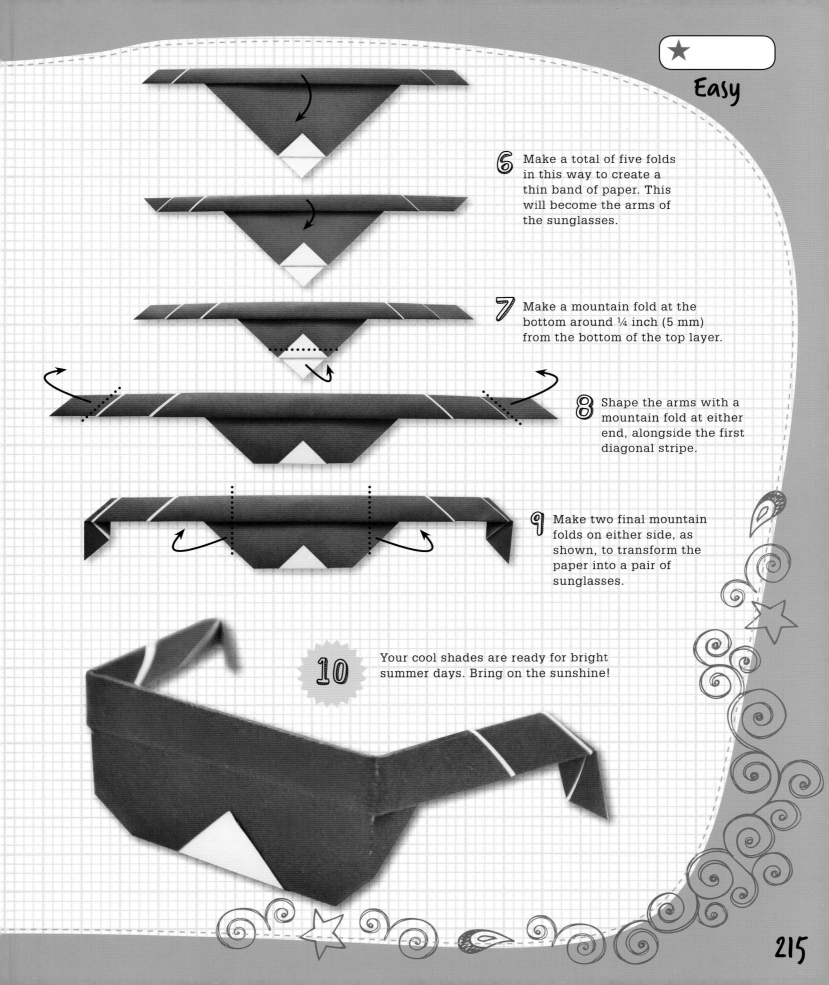

6 Make a total of five folds in this way to create a thin band of paper. This will become the arms of the sunglasses.

7 Make a mountain fold at the bottom around ¼ inch (5 mm) from the bottom of the top layer.

8 Shape the arms with a mountain fold at either end, alongside the first diagonal stripe.

9 Make two final mountain folds on either side, as shown, to transform the paper into a pair of sunglasses.

10 Your cool shades are ready for bright summer days. Bring on the sunshine!

Clutch bag

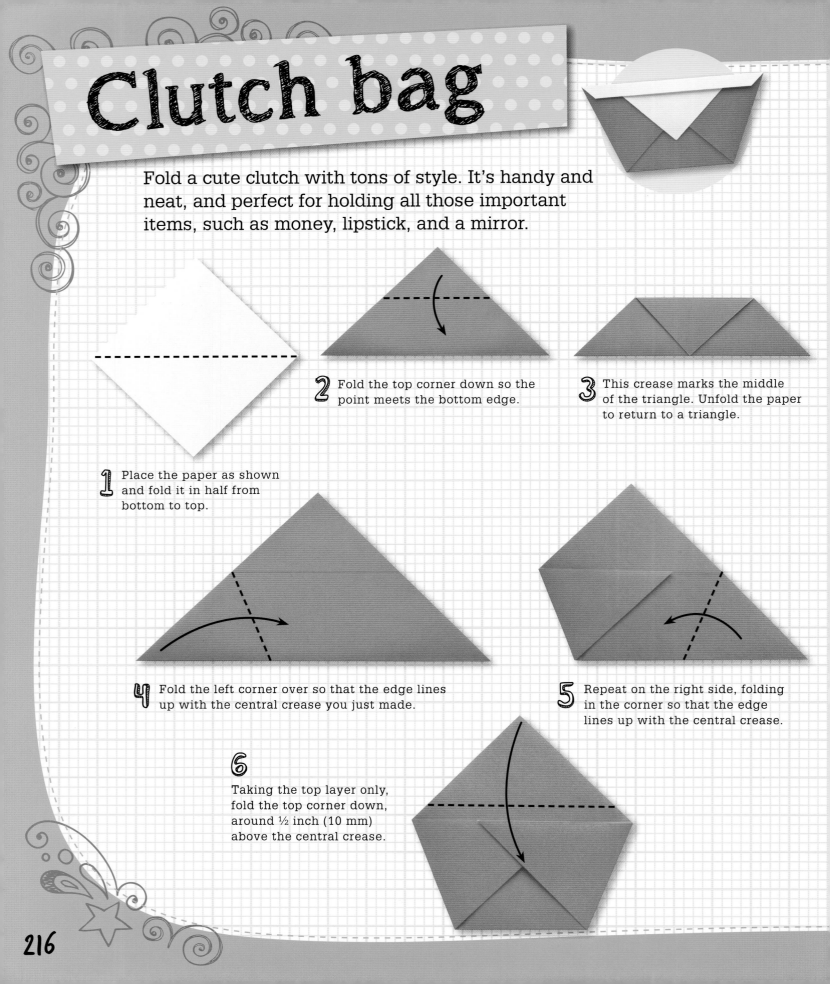

Fold a cute clutch with tons of style. It's handy and neat, and perfect for holding all those important items, such as money, lipstick, and a mirror.

2 Fold the top corner down so the point meets the bottom edge.

3 This crease marks the middle of the triangle. Unfold the paper to return to a triangle.

1 Place the paper as shown and fold it in half from bottom to top.

4 Fold the left corner over so that the edge lines up with the central crease you just made.

5 Repeat on the right side, folding in the corner so that the edge lines up with the central crease.

6 Taking the top layer only, fold the top corner down, around ½ inch (10 mm) above the central crease.

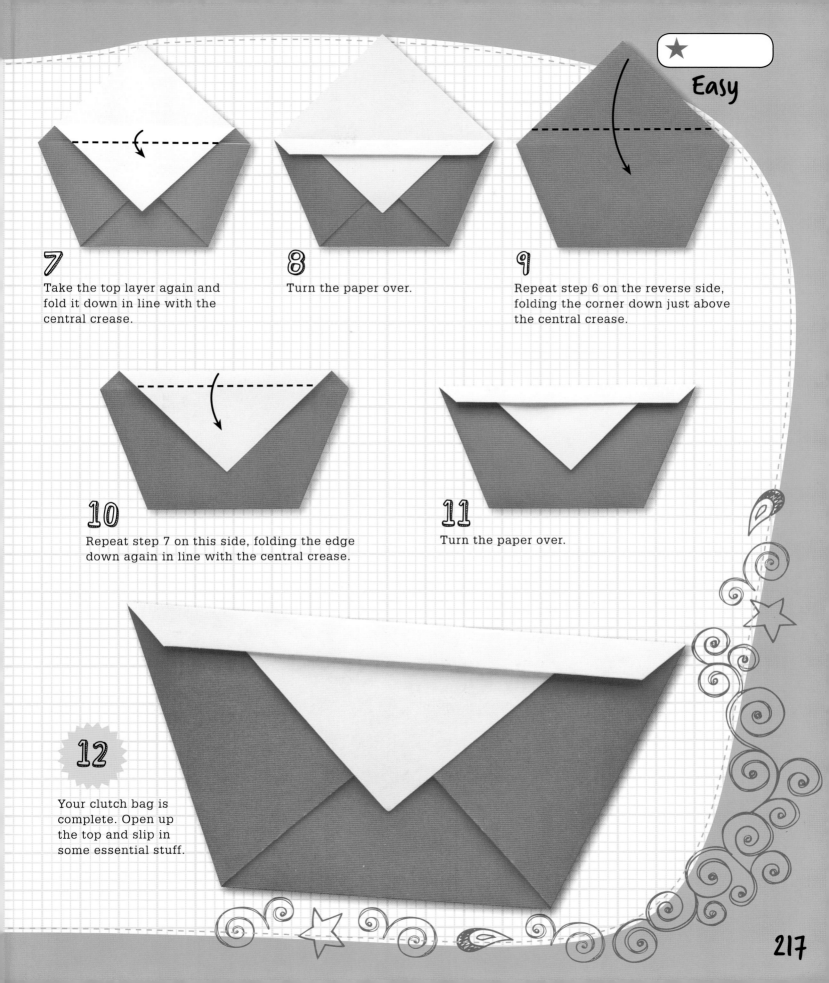

7 Take the top layer again and fold it down in line with the central crease.

8 Turn the paper over.

9 Repeat step 6 on the reverse side, folding the corner down just above the central crease.

10 Repeat step 7 on this side, folding the edge down again in line with the central crease.

11 Turn the paper over.

12 Your clutch bag is complete. Open up the top and slip in some essential stuff.

Bangle

Get ready to roll a fab bangle without the jingle-jangle. Choose a bright paper to create really dazzling diagonal stripes.

1 Place the paper as shown. Fold it in half from top to bottom and unfold, then from left to right and unfold.

2 Valley fold the paper from bottom to top, leaving a ¼ inch (5 mm) border of white around the top edges.

3 Turn the paper over.

4 Fold the bottom edge in again with a valley fold ¼ inch (5 mm) above the central crease.

5 Roll the paper over, creasing the paper next to the fold you just made.

6 Roll over and crease again. You can see the pattern of diagonal stripes beginning to appear at either end.

7
Continue to roll and crease the paper in the same way, pressing down firmly after each roll.

8 When all of the paper is rolled into a band, secure the point with a piece of sticky tape. Bend the ends around and bring them together in a circle. Slide one end between the folds on the other end to hold it in place.

9

Your stripy bangle is finished. You can fold an armful of paper bling that hardly costs a thing!

Socks

Don't worry about odd socks on paper-washing day. Fold lots of pairs, pin them on a line, and watch them flutter in the breeze for fun!

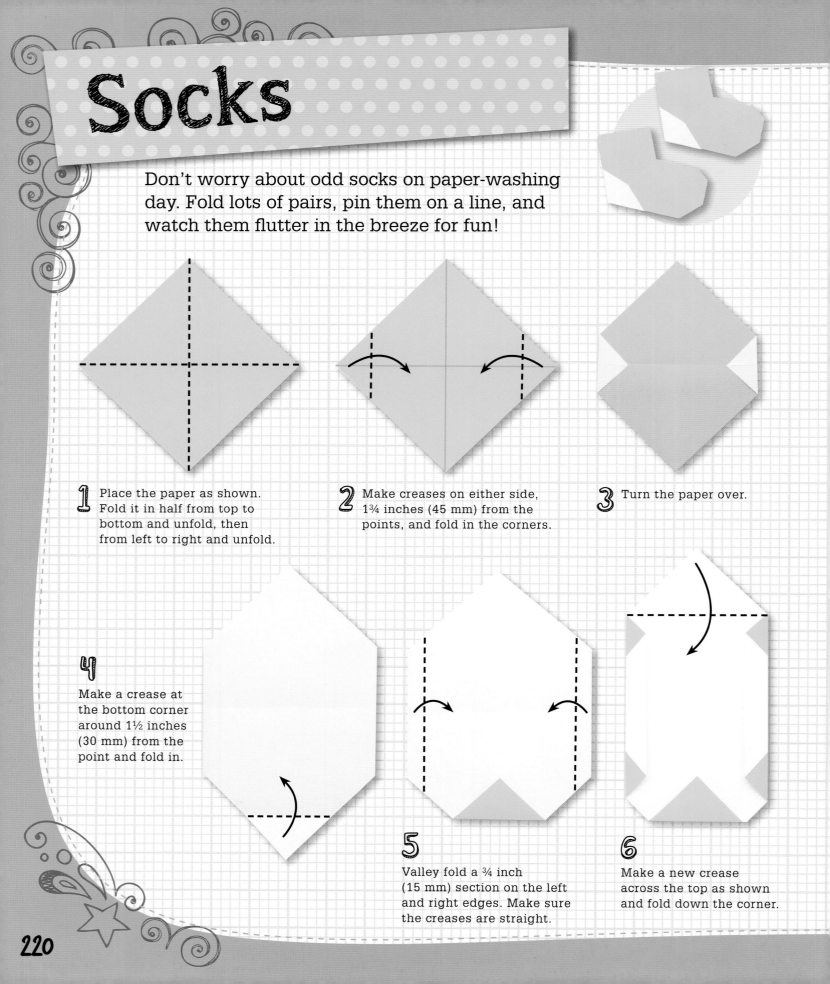

1 Place the paper as shown. Fold it in half from top to bottom and unfold, then from left to right and unfold.

2 Make creases on either side, 1¾ inches (45 mm) from the points, and fold in the corners.

3 Turn the paper over.

4 Make a crease at the bottom corner around 1½ inches (30 mm) from the point and fold in.

5 Valley fold a ¾ inch (15 mm) section on the left and right edges. Make sure the creases are straight.

6 Make a new crease across the top as shown and fold down the corner.

7 Turn the paper over.

8 Fold the paper in half from bottom to top along the central crease.

9 Taking the top layer only, fold the paper in half diagonally from top to bottom as shown.

10 Look carefully and you will see creases across the paper that you made earlier. Mountain fold along these creases.

11 Fold back the top section first to make the upper part of the sock. Then fold down the bottom section, pressing down as shown to make the foot shape.

12 Shape the toe with a mountain fold on the corner.

13 Your ankle sock is finished. Now fold another sock to make a perfect pair.

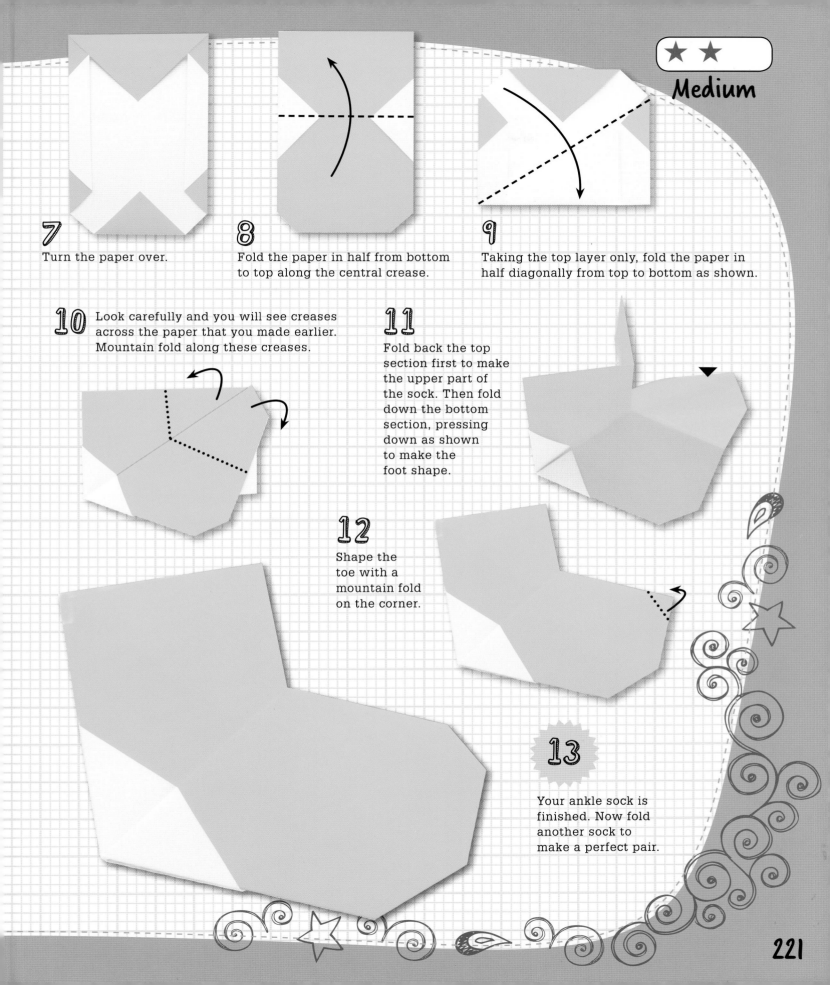

Boots

Footwear doesn't need to be black or brown.
Be bold with red, yellow, or blue, and fold
some trendy heeled boots topped with white trim.

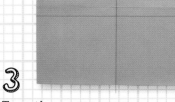

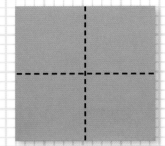

1
Fold the paper from left to right and unfold, then from top to bottom and unfold.

2
Make a crease around 1 inch (25 mm) from the top edge and fold the paper over.

3
Turn the paper over.

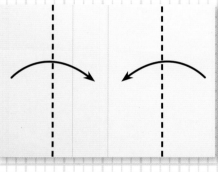

4
Fold the left and right edges in to meet the central crease.

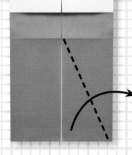

5
On the top layer, make a crease from the middle point to the bottom right corner.

6
Fold the paper over along the crease. Now unfold the left-hand side.

7
Valley fold the paper from the central crease on the left edge to the right edge as shown.

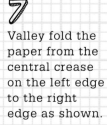

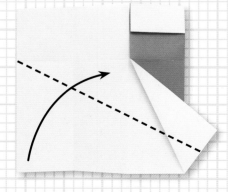

8
Fold over the left side along the crease you made in step 4.
Make a diagonal fold from the bottom of this crease to the right edge, just above the central crease, then unfold.

9
Take the top corner and fold it down along the crease you just made.

10
Fold the left edge over to meet the middle and press the paper flat.

11
Valley fold the tip of the white corner as shown, then fold the paper in half from right to left.

12
Tuck the white band on the right inside the band on the left to secure it.

13
Your boot is nearly finished. Mountain fold the tip of the bottom corner to make the sole.

14
Your boot is now ready. To create a pair, follow the same steps, but make all the folds on the opposite side.

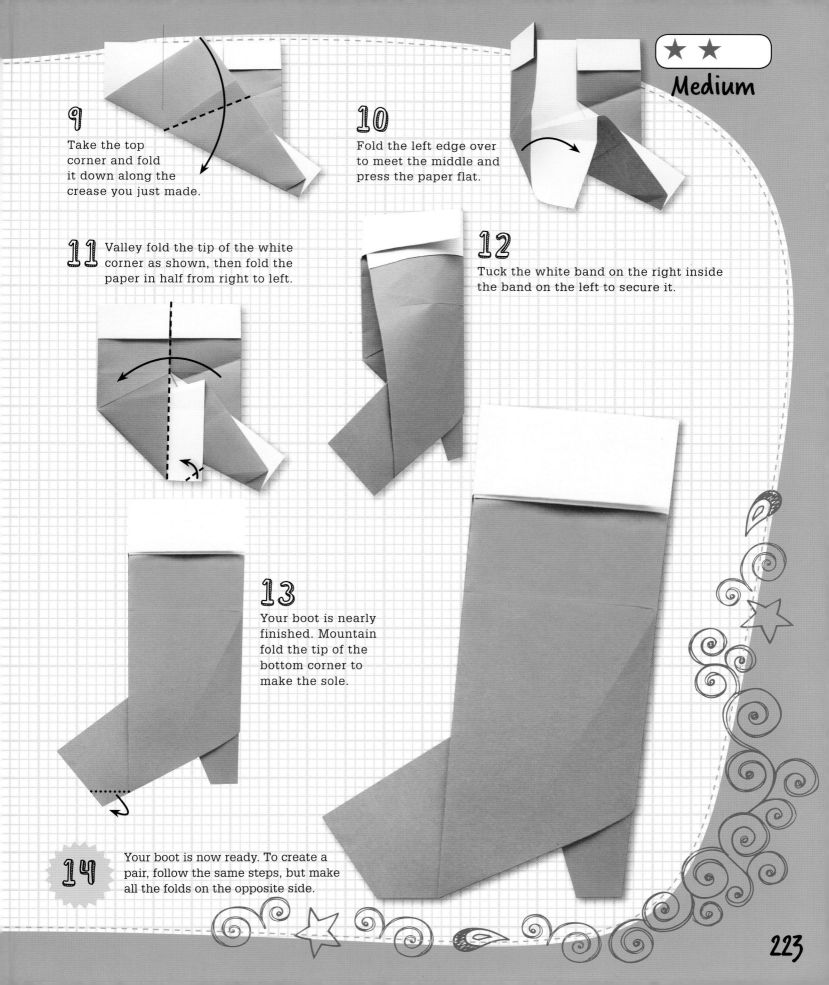

Mittens

It takes some clever folding to create a pair of cozy mittens. Make a beanie hat to match the mitts and you are all ready for a paper snowball fight!

1
Fold the paper in half from top to bottom and unfold. Then from left to right and unfold.

2
Fold the paper in half again from right to left.

3
Taking the top layer only, fold the left edge over to meet the right edge.

4
Make a diagonal crease from the bottom corner as shown. Make another crease that meets it in a "V," then unfold both creases.

5
Take the bottom right corner and pull it up and to the side. Press down on the upper edge, as shown, to make a new crease.

6
Flatten the paper to start off the thumb shape. Now fold down the corner as shown.

7
When you have this shape, open up the paper a little and pull down the corner slightly. Press flat to crease.

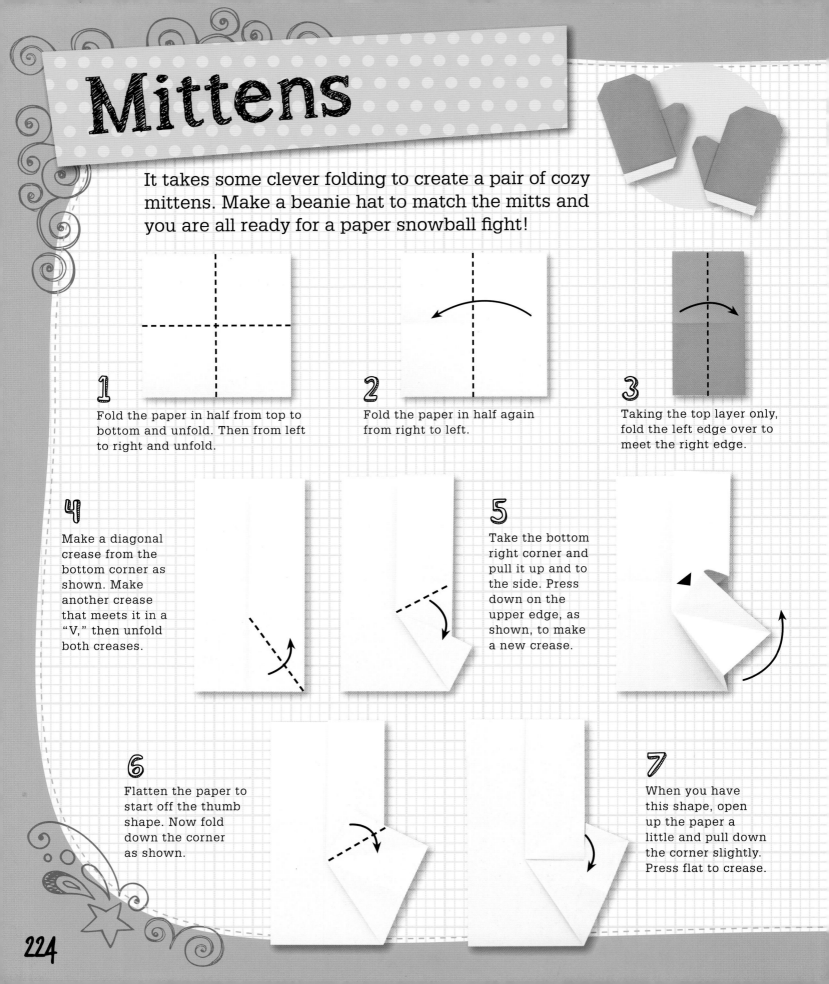

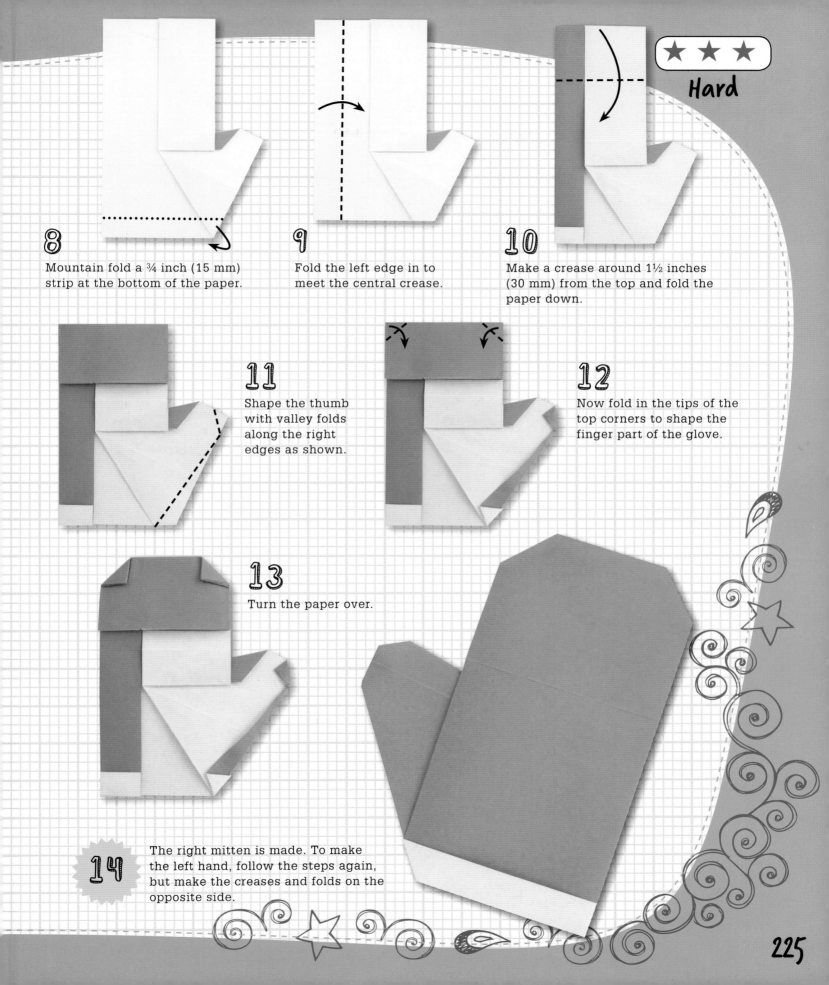

8

Mountain fold a ¾ inch (15 mm) strip at the bottom of the paper.

9

Fold the left edge in to meet the central crease.

10

Make a crease around 1½ inches (30 mm) from the top and fold the paper down.

11

Shape the thumb with valley folds along the right edges as shown.

12

Now fold in the tips of the top corners to shape the finger part of the glove.

13

Turn the paper over.

14

The right mitten is made. To make the left hand, follow the steps again, but make the creases and folds on the opposite side.

Hats

When it comes to folded fashions, hats are hip! Find out how to make a host of headgear, from an easy-peasy beanie to a Stetson straight out of the Wild West.

Howdy partner!

Cowboy hat

Here comes the King!

Crown

Beanie

Pixie hat

Alakazam!

Wizard's hat

227

Beanie

A beanie is the perfect hat to keep your ears warm in cold weather. It's so simple to fold that you can make a different one for every day of the week.

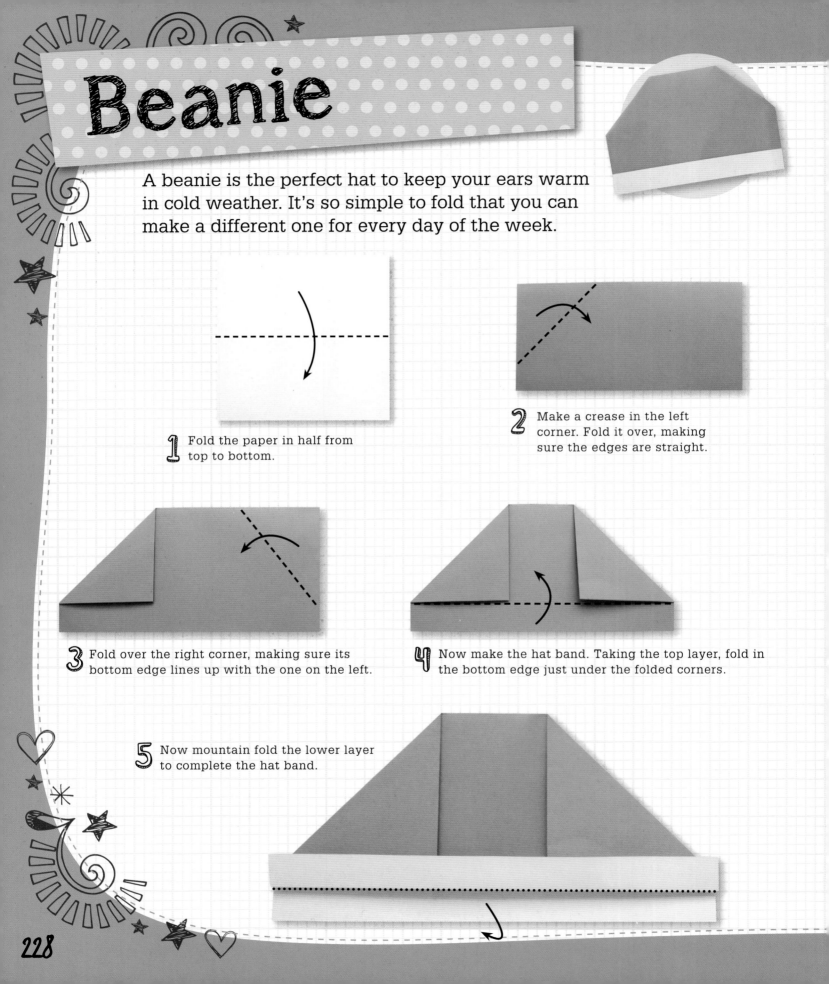

1 Fold the paper in half from top to bottom.

2 Make a crease in the left corner. Fold it over, making sure the edges are straight.

3 Fold over the right corner, making sure its bottom edge lines up with the one on the left.

4 Now make the hat band. Taking the top layer, fold in the bottom edge just under the folded corners.

5 Now mountain fold the lower layer to complete the hat band.

6 Fold in the left-hand point.
Crease firmly.

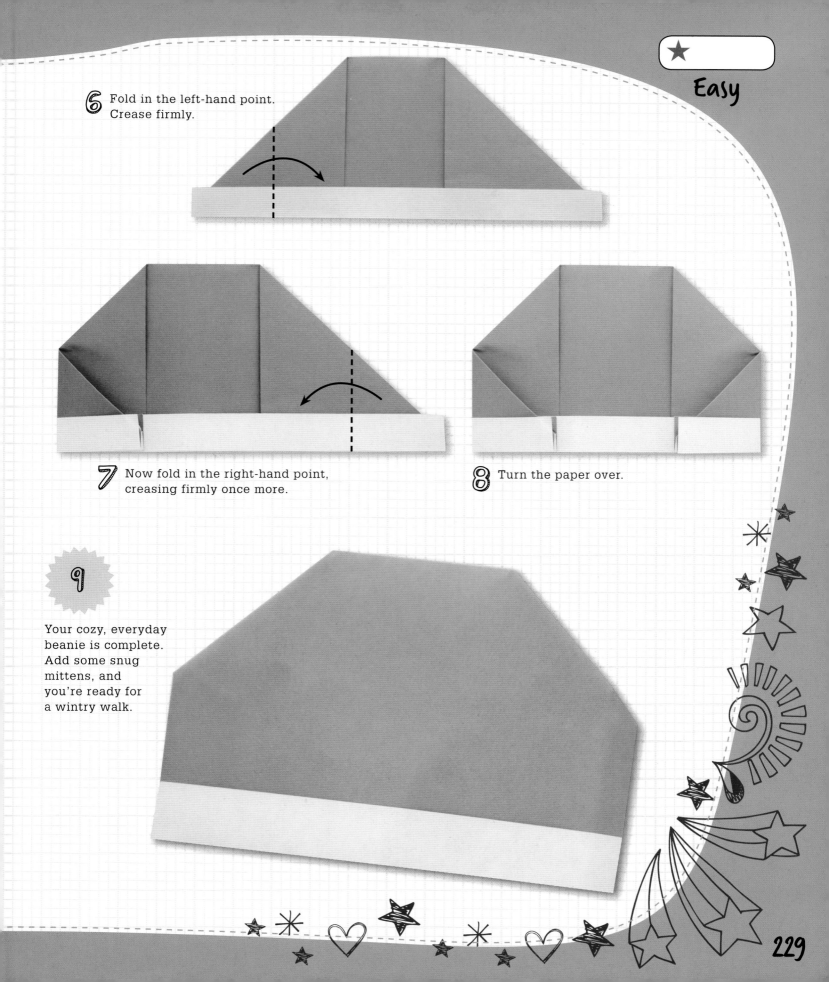

7 Now fold in the right-hand point,
creasing firmly once more.

8 Turn the paper over.

9

Your cozy, everyday
beanie is complete.
Add some snug
mittens, and
you're ready for
a wintry walk.

Crown

This fabulous crown is fit for a king or queen. Use yellow paper that glows like gold and it will sit proudly on any royal head.

1 Place the paper as shown. Fold in half from left to right.

2 Fold in the left and right corners to meet the central crease.

3 Fold in the top and bottom corners in the same way.

4 You should now have a square. Turn the paper over.

5 Fold over the top edge to meet the central crease.

6 Repeat with the bottom edge.

7 Fold in the bottom triangle so the white side is showing.

8 Valley fold the bottom corners to meet the central crease.

9 Fold down both layers of the triangle along the crease you made earlier.

10 Now fold in the top corners to meet the central crease.

11 Fold over the top layer of the triangle to make a square.

12 Hold the top and bottom corners and gently pull the triangles apart.

13 Pinch the creases between your fingers and work around the opening, making it round.

14 Turn your stately crown the right way up. Try adding some sparkling gem stickers for a really regal look.

Wizard's hat

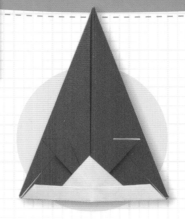

Take a square of paper and conjure up a wizard's pointy hat. You don't need special powers, just a little paper-folding magic!

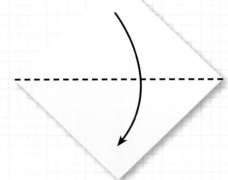

1 Place the paper as shown and fold it in half from top to bottom.

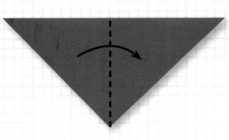

2 Fold it in half from left to right and unfold.

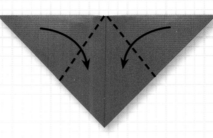

3 Fold in the top points to meet the bottom point. This makes a square.

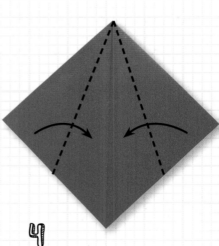

4 Fold in the left and right edges from the top corner to meet the central crease. This makes a kite shape.

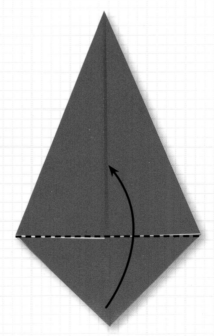

5 Taking the top layers only, fold in the bottom triangles.

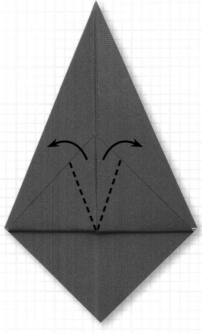

6 Make two angled creases that meet in a "V." Fold over so that the points meet the outer edges.

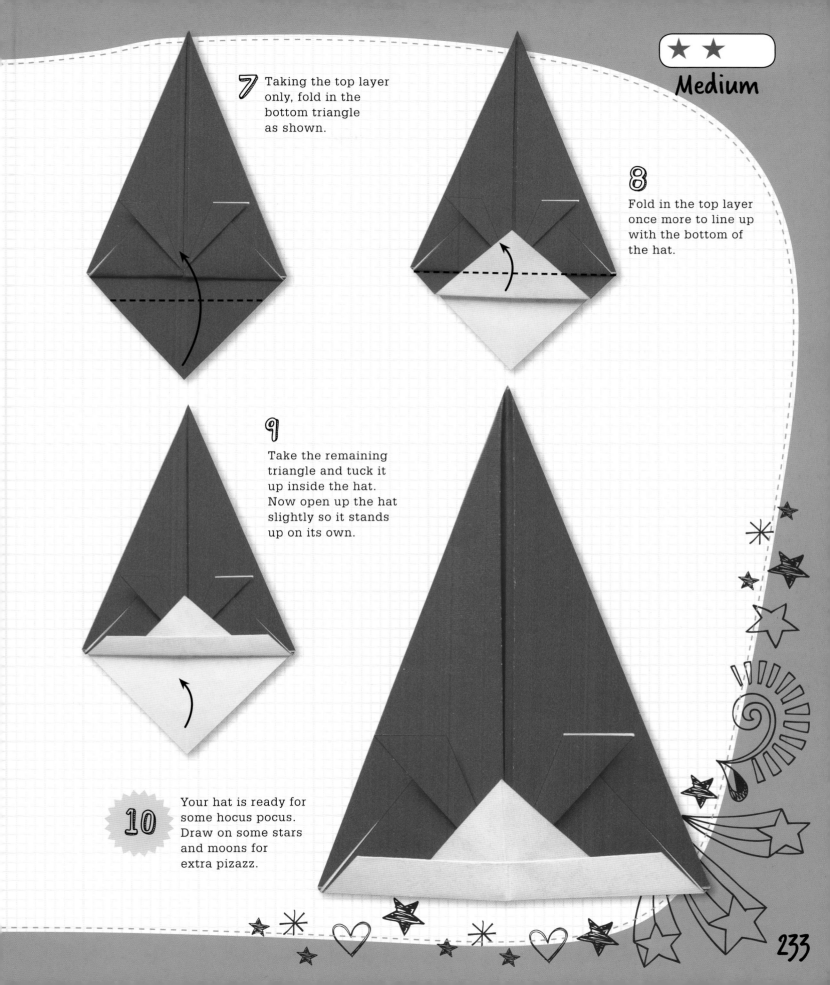

7 Taking the top layer only, fold in the bottom triangle as shown.

8 Fold in the top layer once more to line up with the bottom of the hat.

9 Take the remaining triangle and tuck it up inside the hat. Now open up the hat slightly so it stands up on its own.

10 Your hat is ready for some hocus pocus. Draw on some stars and moons for extra pizazz.

Pixie hat

You could make some mischief with this enchanting pixie hat. Fold it carefully from forest green paper and leave it out for a little person to find!

1 Place the paper as shown and fold it in half from bottom to top.

2 Fold the paper in half from left to right, then unfold.

3 Fold over the left corner. The point should touch the right-hand edge and the top edge should be straight.

4 Repeat with the right corner. The top edges should overlap and line up.

5 Make a crease just above the folded corners. Fold over the top layer of the top corner.

6 Mountain fold the bottom layer.

7 You now have a paper cup. Turn the cup upside down.

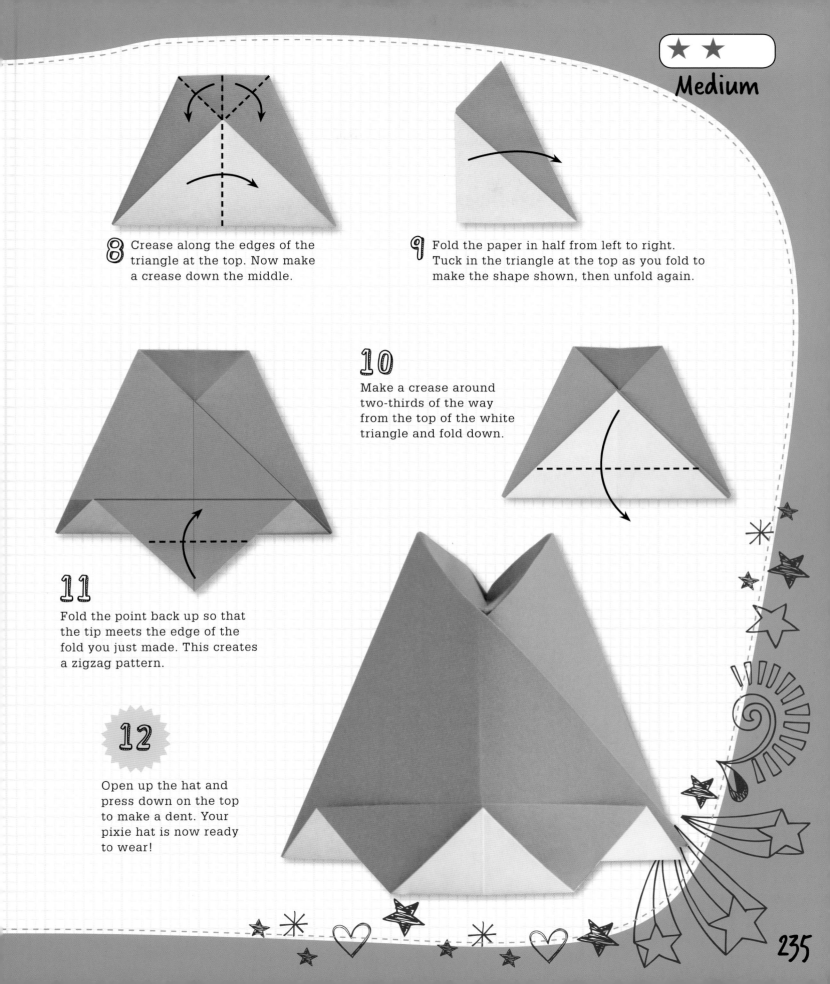

8 Crease along the edges of the triangle at the top. Now make a crease down the middle.

9 Fold the paper in half from left to right. Tuck in the triangle at the top as you fold to make the shape shown, then unfold again.

10 Make a crease around two-thirds of the way from the top of the white triangle and fold down.

11 Fold the point back up so that the tip meets the edge of the fold you just made. This creates a zigzag pattern.

12 Open up the hat and press down on the top to make a dent. Your pixie hat is now ready to wear!

Cowboy hat

No cowboy is complete without his Stetson. It keeps out the sun and the rain on long rides across the prairies, and it looks seriously cool!

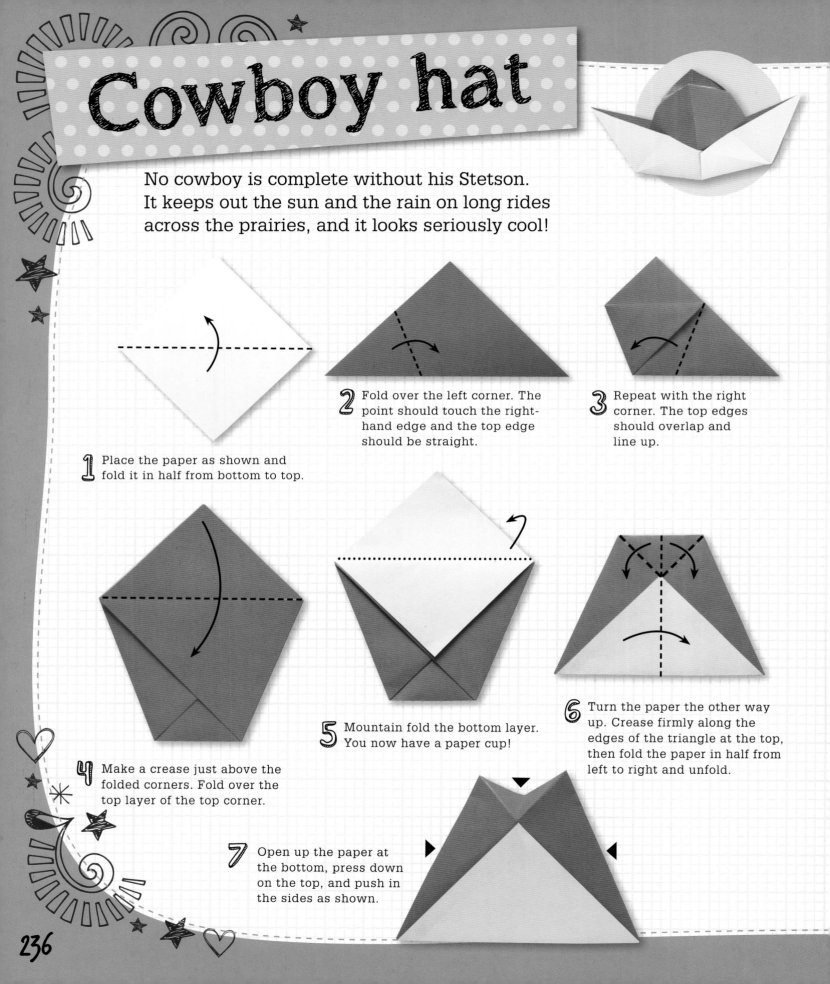

1 Place the paper as shown and fold it in half from bottom to top.

2 Fold over the left corner. The point should touch the right-hand edge and the top edge should be straight.

3 Repeat with the right corner. The top edges should overlap and line up.

4 Make a crease just above the folded corners. Fold over the top layer of the top corner.

5 Mountain fold the bottom layer. You now have a paper cup!

6 Turn the paper the other way up. Crease firmly along the edges of the triangle at the top, then fold the paper in half from left to right and unfold.

7 Open up the paper at the bottom, press down on the top, and push in the sides as shown.

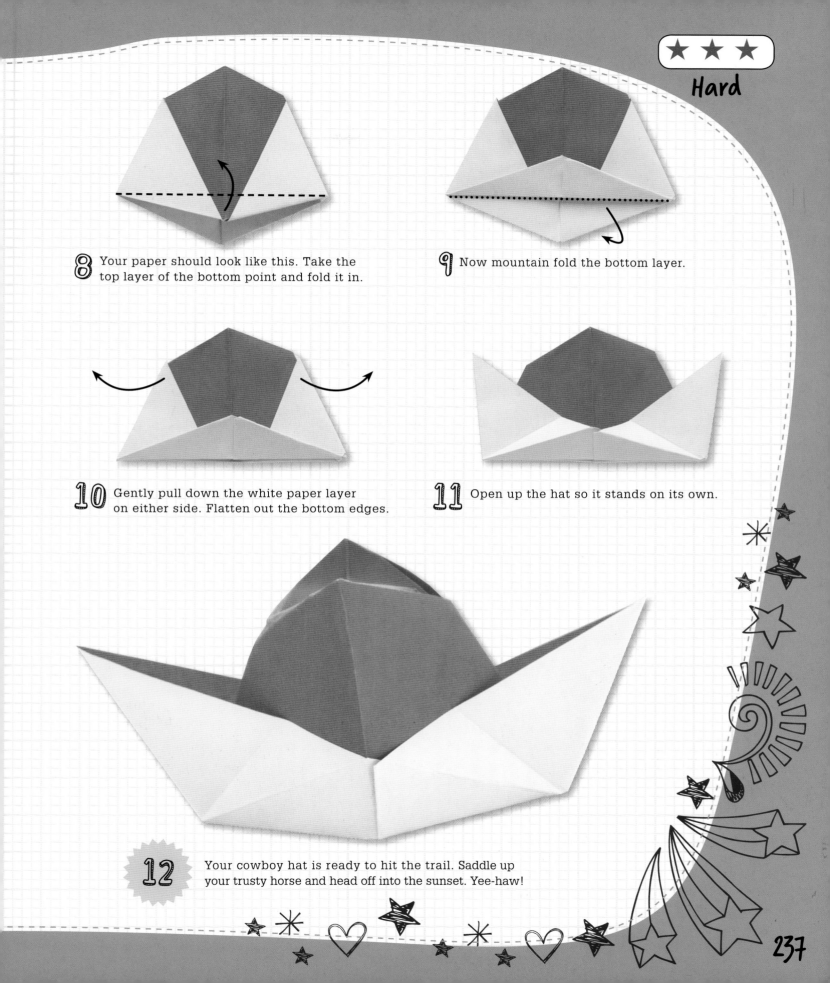

8 Your paper should look like this. Take the top layer of the bottom point and fold it in.

9 Now mountain fold the bottom layer.

10 Gently pull down the white paper layer on either side. Flatten out the bottom edges.

11 Open up the hat so it stands on its own.

12 Your cowboy hat is ready to hit the trail. Saddle up your trusty horse and head off into the sunset. Yee-haw!

Special outfits

There's an outfit to fold for every occasion, whether it's a special ceremony, a dazzling wedding, or just a day at work.

Uniform

Here comes the bride!

Wedding dress

Kimono

Apron

Mmm, what's cooking?

Cheerleader

Go team, go!

Uniform

Fold a smart uniform that works for lots of jobs, from a nurse to a flight attendant. Master the steps and you can kit out a whole workforce!

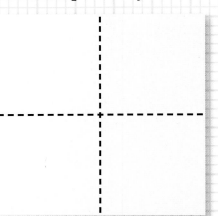

1 Fold the paper from top to bottom and unfold. Then from left to right and unfold.

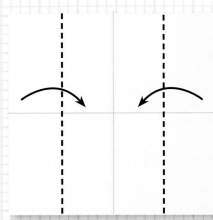

2 Fold the edges in to meet the central crease.

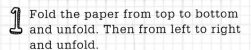

3 To make the collar, make two angled creases that meet in a "V" as shown.

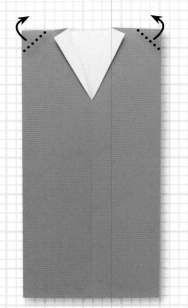

4 Shape the shoulders by mountain folding the tip of the top corners.

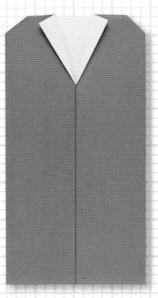

5 Turn the paper over.

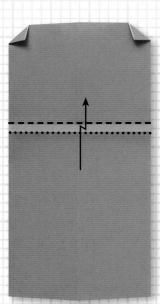

6 Make the waist with a step fold across the middle of the paper.

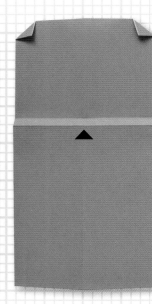

7 Press down on the step fold so that it lies flat.

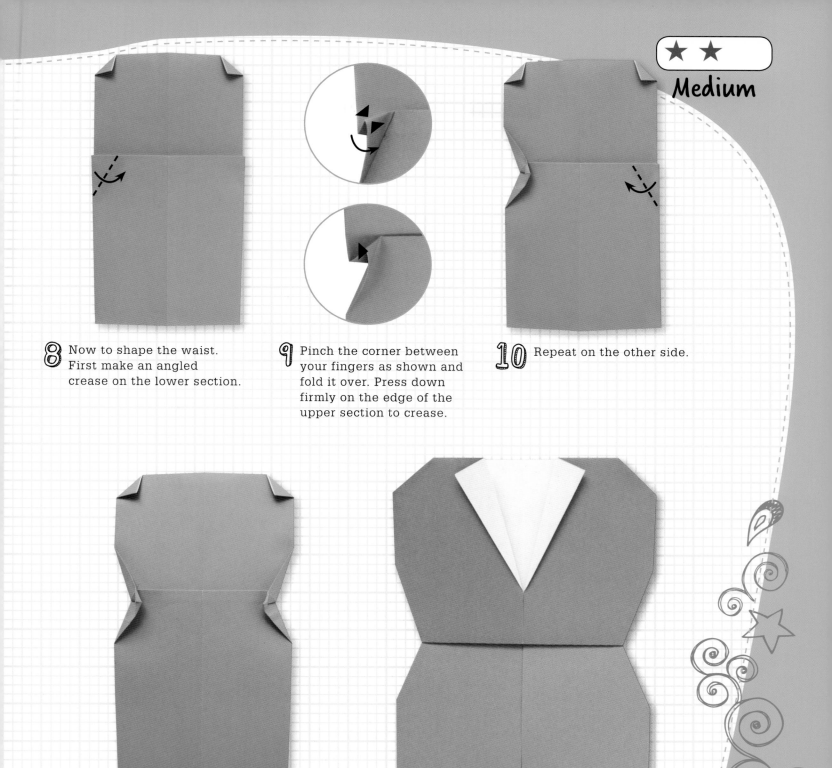

8 Now to shape the waist. First make an angled crease on the lower section.

9 Pinch the corner between your fingers as shown and fold it over. Press down firmly on the edge of the upper section to crease.

10 Repeat on the other side.

11 Turn the paper over to see the finished dress.

12 You now have a neat and tidy uniform ready for duty! Will it be for a nurse to wear on her rounds, or a flight attendant to take to the skies?

241

Cheerleader

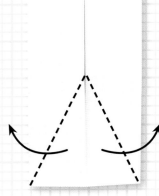

This fun cheerleader dress is a real crowd-pleaser. Pick a bright paper that will really stand out, and prepare to make some noise!

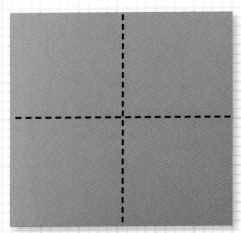

1 Fold the paper from top to bottom and unfold. Then from left to right and unfold.

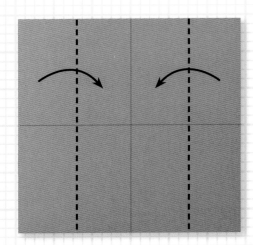

2 Fold the edges in to meet the central crease.

3 Make the skirt by folding over the bottom edges as shown.

4 Make the matching collar with two angled creases that meet in a "V" as shown. Fold down, making sure the edges are even.

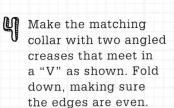

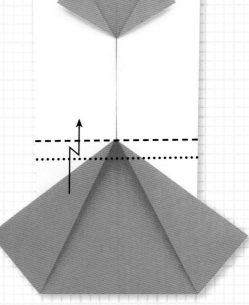

5 Create the waist with a step fold. Start with a valley fold across the central crease.

6 Press down on the step fold
so that it lies flat.

7 Mountain fold ¼ inch (5 mm) from the edge on
either side, keeping the sides straight.

8 Now your eye-catching
cheerleader dress is ready
for action! Entertain the
crowds with some rousing
routines and cheer your
team to victory!

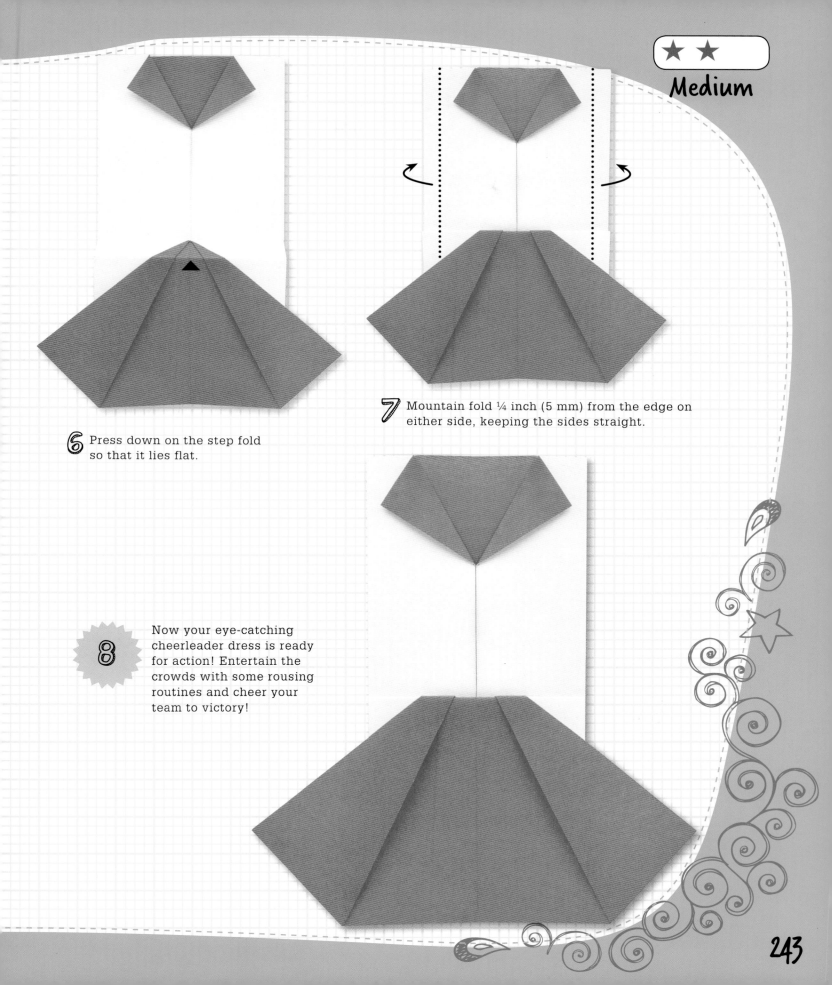

Wedding dress

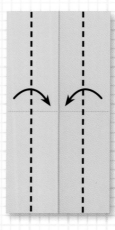

This gorgeous white gown is every bride's dream. With some careful folding you can create a beautiful bodice and a sweeping skirt to make the groom gasp!

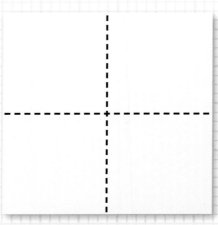

1 Fold the paper from top to bottom and unfold. Then from left to right and unfold.

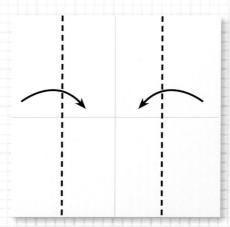

2 Fold the edges in to meet the central crease.

3 Fold the edges in to meet the central crease once more.

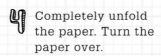

4 Completely unfold the paper. Turn the paper over.

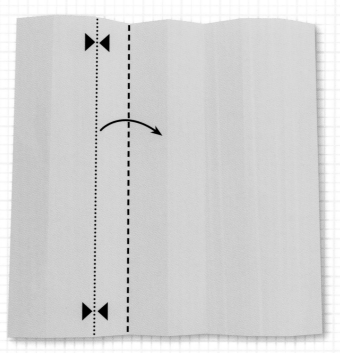

5 Now make a pleat. Take the second crease from the left to meet the central crease. Press flat.

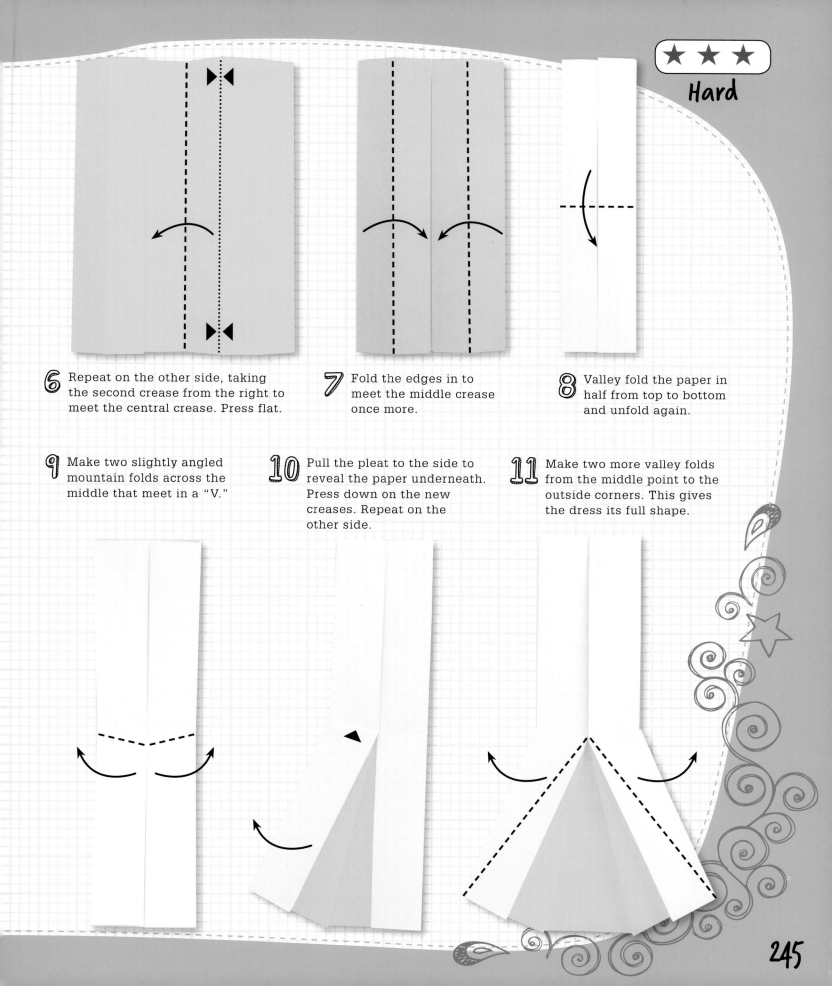

6 Repeat on the other side, taking the second crease from the right to meet the central crease. Press flat.

7 Fold the edges in to meet the middle crease once more.

8 Valley fold the paper in half from top to bottom and unfold again.

9 Make two slightly angled mountain folds across the middle that meet in a "V."

10 Pull the pleat to the side to reveal the paper underneath. Press down on the new creases. Repeat on the other side.

11 Make two more valley folds from the middle point to the outside corners. This gives the dress its full shape.

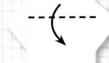

12 Make two angled creases from the top corners that meet in a "V" as shown.

13 Fold along these creases to make the sleeve shapes. Turn the paper over.

14 Now for the neck. Make a valley fold around ¾ inch (15 mm) from the top edge.

15 Put your finger on the lower layer of the pleat. Press down on the creases on either side to flatten them into triangular shapes.

16 Now open up the neck with two angled mountain folds as shown.

17 Valley fold the bottom edge of the neck to neaten it up.

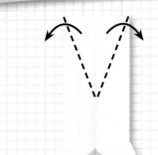

18

Create the waist
with a step fold.
Start with a valley
fold across the
central crease.

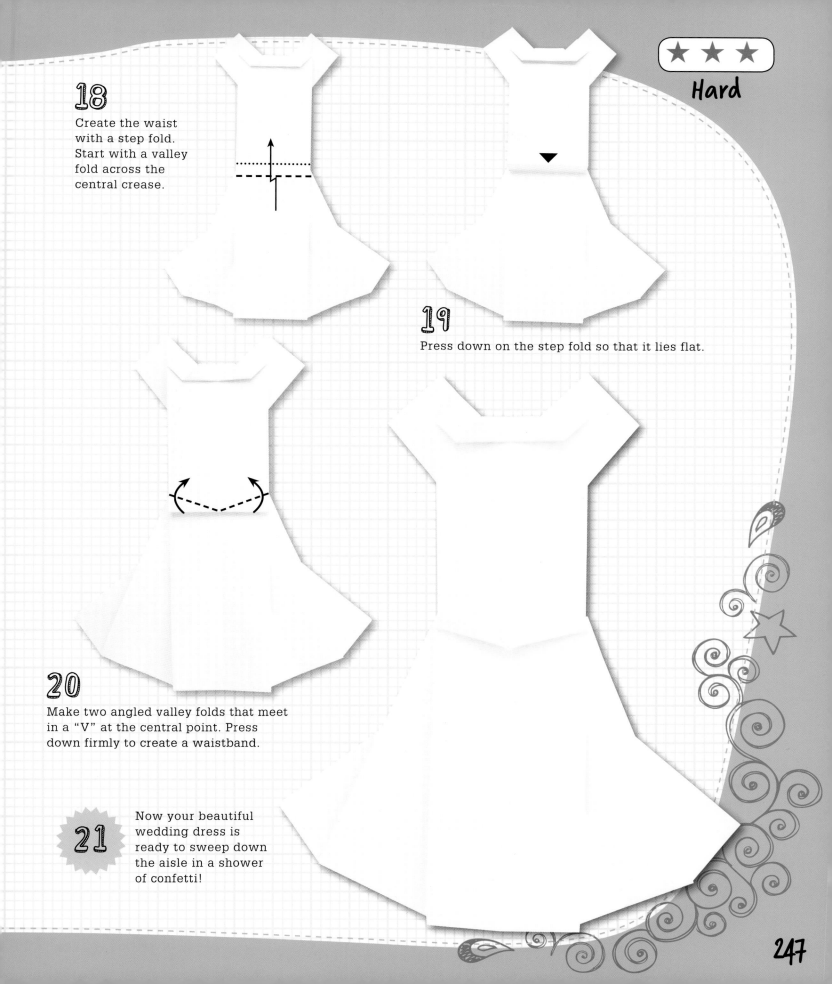

19

Press down on the step fold so that it lies flat.

20

Make two angled valley folds that meet
in a "V" at the central point. Press
down firmly to create a waistband.

21

Now your beautiful
wedding dress is
ready to sweep down
the aisle in a shower
of confetti!

Kimono

Follow the steps to turn an ordinary square of paper into an amazing, oriental robe. Deep red is the perfect shade for this traditional Japanese costume.

1
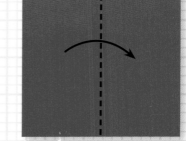
Fold the paper in half from left to right and unfold.

2
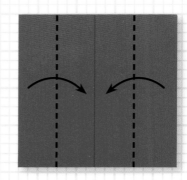
Fold the edges in to meet the central crease.

3
Unfold the paper and turn it over.

4
Now make a pleat. Take the first crease on the left to meet the central crease. Press flat.

5
Repeat on the other side, taking the first crease on the right to meet the central crease. Press flat.

6
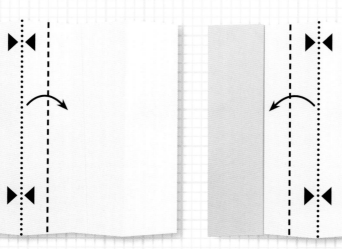
You should now have a pleat down the middle of the paper, like this.

8 Make a step fold as shown. When it is pressed flat, the step fold should touch the paper just below the folded top edge.

7 Make a valley fold about ½ inch (10 mm) from the top edge.

9 Make the collar by opening up the pleat at the top. Put your finger on the lower layer, then press down on the creases on either side to flatten them into triangular shapes.

10 Make a step fold in the top half of the collar.

11 Make a crease down the left side from the edge of the collar.

Kimono

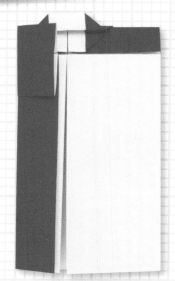

12 Fold firmly along the new crease and unfold again.

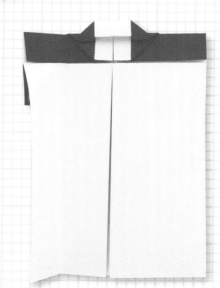

13 To make the first sleeve, open up the corner of the lower section.

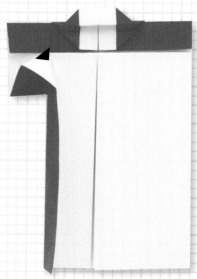

14 Push down on the crease that runs along the top and press it flat, folding in the edge of the paper as you go.

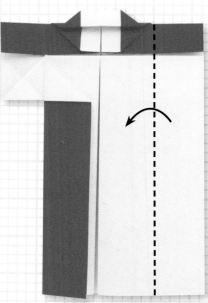

15 Now make a crease down the right side from the edge of the collar.

16 Fold firmly along the new crease, then unfold again.

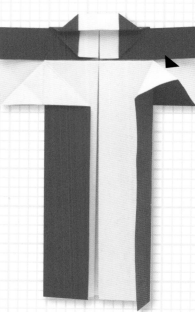

17 Open up the corner, as before, and press it flat to make the other sleeve.

18 Make an angled crease below the sleeve, as shown, and fold over.

19 Crease and fold the right-hand side in the same way to make the flared robe.

20 Valley fold the tips of the sleeves.

21 Turn the paper over to see the finished garment.

22 Take a bow! Your Japanese kimono is ready for a special occasion, like a tea party or a wedding.

Apron

Roll up your sleeves and prepare for some fancy folding to create this pretty apron. All you need are nimble fingers and a square of paper!

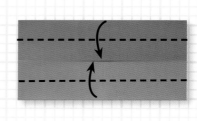

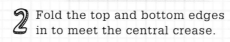

1 Fold the paper from top to bottom and unfold. Then from left to right and unfold.

2 Fold the top and bottom edges in to meet the central crease.

3 Fold the top and bottom edges in to meet the central crease once more.

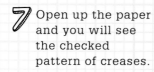

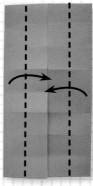

4 Open up the paper.

5 With the creases running across, fold the left and right edges in to meet the central crease.

6 Repeat once more, folding the edges in to meet the central crease.

7 Open up the paper and you will see the checked pattern of creases.

8 Turn the paper over.

9 Fold in the left edge to meet the first crease. Repeat on the other side.

10 Now fold up the bottom edge to meet the first crease from the bottom.

11 Turn the paper over.

12 Fold in the sides along the second crease from each edge.

13 Turn the paper over.

14 Fold down the top edge along the first crease.

15 To make the neck, open up the top left corner and press down on the crease to flatten it into a triangular shape. Repeat on the other side.

Apron

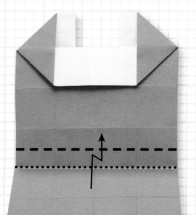

16 Make the waist with a step fold across the middle of the dress.

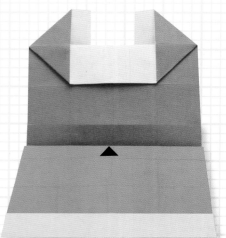

17 Press down on the step fold so that it lies flat.

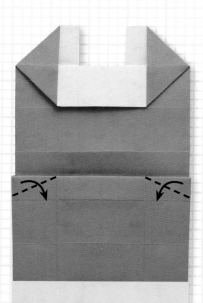

18 Make two angled creases at the corners of the step fold as shown.

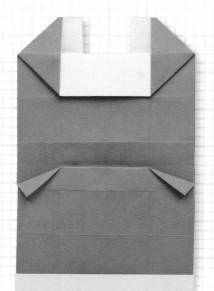

19 Fold and crease firmly, then unfold.

20 Turn the paper over.

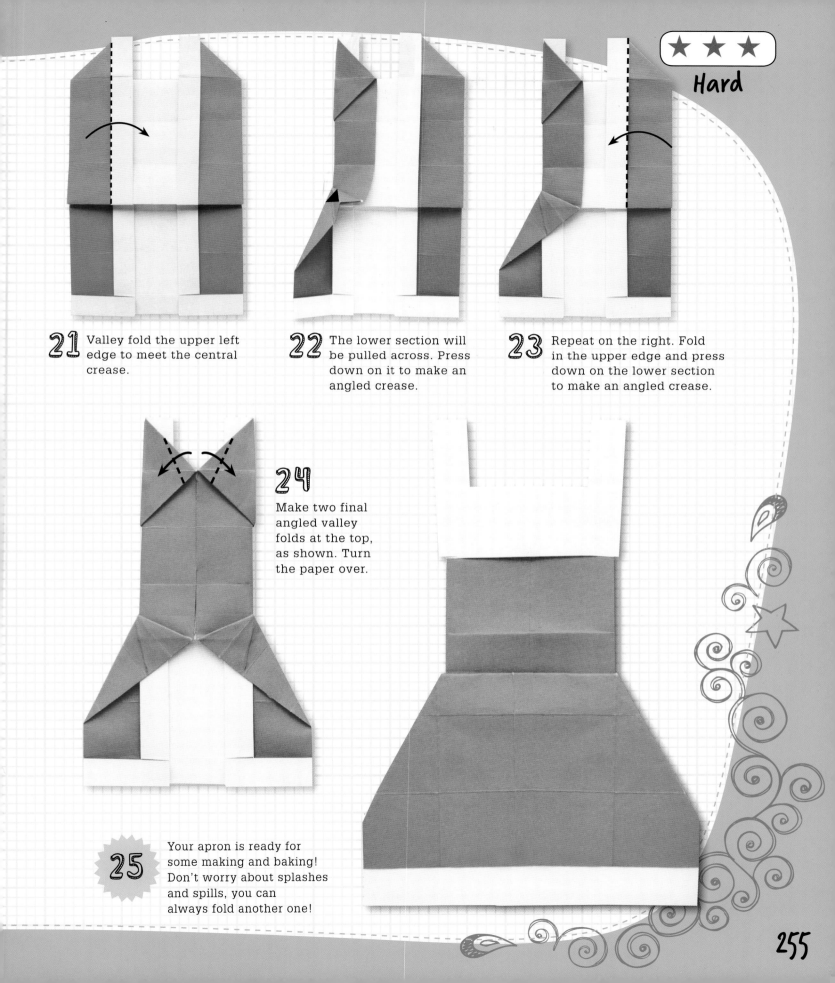

21 Valley fold the upper left edge to meet the central crease.

22 The lower section will be pulled across. Press down on it to make an angled crease.

23 Repeat on the right. Fold in the upper edge and press down on the lower section to make an angled crease.

24 Make two final angled valley folds at the top, as shown. Turn the paper over.

25 Your apron is ready for some making and baking! Don't worry about splashes and spills, you can always fold another one!

Fashion show

Now that you have created a fabulous collection of paper clothes, try your hand at becoming a top fashion stylist. Put together some gorgeous outfits to suit every occasion.

Mix and match tops, skirts, and shorts, try out shoes and hats, then throw in some cute accessories to complete each look!

Party on

Look smart

Wrap up

Stay cool